Book A

ALLAHABAD, India, Chronicle Foreign Service---A 27-
ear-old peasant is wandering the streets of Indian towns be-
use no one wants to give her shelter. There are thousands of
oor begging in this country, but Rasmanjari Rani is unwanted
r a strange reason.

Rasmanjari is nearly nine feet tall---one of the tallest women in the world.

When she went to a poor house the other day, the priest locked the door after one look at her.

"Maybe he thought I was a witch," the dark-eyed woman said. Without any hate she told about her experiences.

Until three years before, Rasmanjari was of normal height. She had been married for many years. There were no children, but she and her husband were happy.

Suddenly, Rasmanjari started growing taller. In two or three months, she added four to five inches to her height. "Everyone in the village saw the change. I was stared at and made fun of. When I went to shop, children would follow me chanting, 'Tall woman, tall woman, you are like the mango tree.' I was

COAL MINER'S DAUGHTER

OW DOES FOLK SINGER LORETTA LYNN FEEL ABOUT THE PEOPLE FROM "BACK HOME"?

FROM HERO TO HEROIN

WHY DID EVERYONE BELIEVE IT COULDN'T HAPPEN TO CLINT DICKENS?

HARRISBURG, Pa. (AP) ---Clint Dickens was a heroin addict. When they found out, a lot of people still could not believe it. When they heard about the lies, when they saw the broken body, their words went something like this: "He's the last kid you would have thought . . ."

At McCaskey High School in nearby Lancaster, Dickens had been a school hero. He was president of the student body and an all-star football

GLOBE BOOK COMPANY, INC.
New York Chicago Dallas

and red-colored food. The man from Alaska soon turned back to his original color.

FROM HERO TO HEROIN

WHY DID EVERYONE BELIEVE IT COULDN'T HAPPEN TO CLINT DICKENS?

HARRISBURG, Pa. (AP) —Clint Dickens was a heroin addict. When they found out, a lot of people still could not

four to five inches to her height. "Everyone in the village saw the change. I was stared at and made fun of. When I went to shop, children would follow me chanting, 'Tall woman, tall woman, you are like the mango tree.' I was even stoned once by some old women."

By last year Rasmanjari was almost nine feet tall. There was no end to the poor woman's bad luck. Her husband had left her. Her brothers' wives turned against her. They said that she was evil. They blamed the death of a child in the family on her. One night she took what she owned and began wandering.

Doctors said she had an illness in the part of the body that controls growth. They said there was no cure. "The doctors do not think I will live

Continued on Page 18, Col. 2

At 6 feet 2 and 210 pounds.

show will go to the wives and children of 38 miners killed two months ago in a mine explosion.

Loretta Lynn still talks and sings with a strong mountain accent. She wrote a hit song, "Coal Miner's Daughter." That song is the story of her own early life in Kentucky.

"I grew up in Butcher Holler," she said. "My daddy was a coal miner for 16 years. My husband worked the mines for a while and his daddy was a miner for 45 years.

"A lot of my friends were killed in the mines. I've walked past where they were bringing out the men. There had been an accident. I remember

real stories

book A

Milton Katz

Michael Chakeres Murray Bromberg

ISBN: 0-87065-202-8

Edited by Martin Apter
Illustrations by Harry J. Schaare
Cover design by Lawrence Schaeffer
Text design by Edward Zytko

PRINTED IN THE UNITED STATES OF AMERICA

7 8 9

ABOUT THE AUTHORS

MILTON KATZ, the chairman of English at Thomas Jefferson High School, Brooklyn, N.Y., has been a high school reading coordinator and a program writer for the Responsive Environment Center. He was the editor of *Moonlight Review,* a national teachers' literary magazine.

MICHAEL CHAKERES, a reading consultant in New York City's High School Reading Program, was formerly laboratory supervisor and coordinator of the Responsive Environment Program.

MURRAY BROMBERG has taught English and been Chairman of English at Thomas Jefferson High School, Brooklyn, New York. Mr. Bromberg has also taught at Hofstra University. Now principal of Andrew Jackson High School, Queens, New York, he is a contributing author of several Globe books. He has also published articles in *Shakespeare Quarterly* and other periodicals.

ACKNOWLEDGMENTS

For permission to reprint copyrighted materials, grateful acknowledgment is made to the following publishers and news services:

"Ice Cream Sodas the Caribbean Way" reprinted with permission of Eastern Airlines, Inc.

"How Sweet the Smell of a Sweet-Smelling Bus" reprinted with permission of The Associated Press.

"Dancing for Rain" reprinted with permission of the *St. Petersburg Times*.

"The Stolen Car" reprinted with permission of the *Denver Post*.

"Orange People" reprinted with permission from SCIENCE NEWS, the weekly magazine of science and the applications of science, copyright 1966 by Science Service, Inc.

"Ask Ann" reprinted with permission of Ann Landers, Publishers-Hall Syndicate, and the *Lancaster New Era*.

"Don't Smoke, Joe" reprinted with permission of The Associated Press.

"Youths Clean Creeks" reprinted with permission of the *Atlanta Constitution*.

"Young, but Old" reprinted with permission of the *St. Louis Post-Dispatch*.

"A Short Honeymoon" reprinted with permission of the *Louisville Courier-Journal*.

"Was It Worth It?" copyright © 1970, (1971) Newsday, Inc. Reprinted by permission.

"All's Well That Ends Well" reprinted with permission of the *Amsterdam News*.

"The Man Who Tried to Fly," copyright © 1971 by the *London Observer*. Reprinted with permission of the Los Angeles Times/Washington Post News Service.

"His Last Trip" reprinted with permission of the *Milwaukee Journal.*

"He'd Rather Sweep Floors," copyright © 1970, 1971, *Los Angeles Times.* Reprinted by permission.

"Undercover Policeman Loses Friends," copyright © 1970, 1971, *Los Angeles Times.* Reprinted by permission.

"Blue Sky Over Tokyo" reprinted by permission from TIME, The Weekly Newsmagazine. Copyright © 1971 Time, Inc.

"Did You Have a Happy Childhood?" reprinted with permission of Chronicle Publishing Co., 1971.

"Two Saved by Teenager," copyright © 1970, (1971) Newsday, Inc. Reprinted by permission.

"WGN Presents . . . A Live Bank Robbery" reprinted with permission of The Associated Press.

"Kiss the Ref," copyright © 1970, 1971, *Los Angeles Times.* Reprinted by permission.

"Do Clothes Make the Man?" reprinted with permission of the *Denver Post.*

"Coal Miner's Daughter" reprinted with permission of the *Louisville Courier-Journal.*

"Crisis Center" reprinted with permission of the *Louisville Courier-Journal.*

"Uganda Basketball Coach," copyright © 1970, 1971, *Los Angeles Times.* Reprinted by Permission.

"Nine-Foot Woman" reprinted with permission of Chronicle Publishing Co., Inc.

"A Man with a Heart" reprinted with permission of the *Louisville Courier-Journal.*

"Bear Killed to Save Man," copyright © 1971 by the New York Times Company. Reprinted by permission.

"Supermex" reprinted by permission from TIME, The Weekly Newsmagazine. Copyright © 1971 Time, Inc.

"From Hero to Heroin" reprinted with permission of the *Lancaster New Era.*

CONTENTS

ABOUT THE BOOK

REAL STORIES, BOOK A, has something for everyone.

For those who like to read about unusual people, there are stories about an orange man and a nine-foot woman. There are also strange stories about an Englishman who tried to fly without a plane, a Brazilian boy who died of old age, and a beautiful American girl who is a basketball referee.

For those who like stories with suspense, there's one about a young man who saved the lives of two men in the same week. You can also read about how people's lives are saved by a "crisis center." Then there's the unusual tale of a live radio broadcast of a bank robbery—with the robber himself being interviewed!

If you like sports, you can read about what it's like to be a basketball coach in Uganda. If you like to laugh, there's a story about a perfumed bus. If you crave excitement, you shouldn't miss the tale of the polar bear who wouldn't let go. And if you are into what's happening now, there are stories about a football star's battle with heroin, a big city's problems with pollution, and a black man's decision to fight for his rights.

These are just some of the unusual and interesting stories you will find in this book. However, the amazing thing is that all of them are true. Each story is an accurate report of something that actually happened. Each story in REAL STORIES is *real* indeed.

1. ICE CREAM SODAS THE CARIBBEAN WAY

ON A HOT SUMMER DAY CARIBBEAN KIDS GET THIRSTY

DO THEY GO TO THE CANDY STORE FOR A SODA?

On a hot day, when Caribbean * *kids* get *thirsty,* they *shinny* to the top of a *coconut palm.*

* Caribbean – an area around the Caribbean sea, with such islands as Haiti, Cuba, Jamaica, and the countries of Central America.

There they reach the *ripest* coconut. They cut it *loose* and let it fall to the ground.

Then they find a rock and they *smash*, smash, smash at the hard coconut skin until they get to the inside *skin*. They call the inside skin the monkey face because it is covered all over with fuzz.

Then they smash harder, harder, harder! They're getting very thirsty now.

At last they find what they have worked so hard for.

Cool, cool coconut milk!

Aah! That's ice cream soda the Caribbean way!

—EASTERN AIRLINES AD, NEW YORK TIMES

CHECK YOUR UNDERSTANDING

1. The kids open coconuts with
   (a) a knife.
   (b) a saw.
   (c) a rock.
2. The kids climb palms for coconuts because they are
   (a) hungry.
   (b) angry.
   (c) thirsty.
3. When the kids *shinny* they
   (a) climb a tree.
   (b) cut down a tree.
   (c) break coconuts.
4. Having ice cream sodas the Caribbean way is:
   (a) breaking coconuts.
   (b) going up trees.
   (c) getting milk from coconuts.
5. Another title that would best explain the main idea of this story is:

(a) Climbing Trees
(b) How to Smash a Coconut
(c) A Cooling Drink in the Caribbean

FIND THE MISSING WORD

In your notebook, complete the following sentences with words from the story. You may look back at the story.

1. On a hot day, Caribbean kids are . . . .
2. They . . . . up a coconut palm.
3. The kids find the . . . . coconut on the palm.
4. They cut it . . . .
5. They . . . . at the hard coconut.

FIRST THINGS FIRST

Arrange these events in the order in which they really happened.

1. The kids shinny up a coconut palm on a hot day.
2. The kids find a rock to smash the outside skin of the coconut.
3. The kids cut loose the ripest coconut.
4. The kids find cool milk.
5. The kids reach the inside skin of the coconut and smash it.

IMPROVING YOUR VOCABULARY

Fill in the blank space in each sentence with the word from Column B that best fits there. Use each word in Column B only once.

A	B
1. Rosa and I were ...., so we stopped for a drink.	(a) skin
2. The water felt good against my	(b) smash
3. It was so .... we had to wear coats.	(c) thirsty
4. We had to .... the window to get into the house.	(d) cool
5. After Lulu's diet, her clothes were .... on her.	(e) loose

---

WORD BUILDING

Alphabetical Order

A. Put these words in alphabetical order. If you get 100% correct, you may skip the next exercise.

hot	fuzz
kids	thirsty
coconut	fall
palm	loose
repeat	worked

B. If you did not get 100%, put these words in alphabetical order. Get 100% and skip the next exercise.

kids	smash
they	inside
hot	Caribbean
milk	reach
fuzz	ground

C. More Practice. Try these ten words.

smash	way
milk	ripest
cut	when
harder	bunch
loose	palm

EXPRESSING YOURSELF

1. This story tells you step-by-step how Caribbean kids get milk from a coconut. You tell the steps you would take to do one of the following:

(a) frying an egg
(b) teaching someone how to ride a bike
(c) teaching someone how to sew a hem
(d) crossing a busy street when the traffic lights are not working

2. Act out one of these in front of your class without saying a word:

(a) Sneaking into your classroom without your teacher seeing you.
(b) Walking on a high wire 100 feet off the ground.
(c) Eating a large hero sandwich.

3. Write a paragraph using one of the following as your first sentence:

(a) Man, was I thirsty!
(b) .... is one country I'd like to visit.
(c) It was a very hot day.

2. HOW SWEET THE SMELL OF A SWEET-SMELLING BUS

A NOTED MAN HAS SAID, "OUR CITIES ARE DYING." CAN WE SAVE THEM?

WHAT DID ONE COMPANY DO TO HELP MAKE THE CITY A BETTER PLACE TO LIVE?

SAN DIEGO, Cal. (AP) – Many car drivers and bus riders *complained* of the strong smell of bus *oil* on the road.

"From now on," said the *manager* of the bus *company*, "the *gas* from our buses will smell as sweet as baby *powder*." Nobody believed him. Who ever heard of a sweet-smelling bus?

But something called Malabate did the job. It was put into the *fuel* of 228 city buses.

A *waitress* took a *sniff* of a passing bus. "It smells like a bus with *perfume* on, honey," said she.

—SAN FRANCISCO CHRONICLE

CHECK YOUR UNDERSTANDING

1. The bus company did something about the problem of the
   (a) powder.
   (b) oil smells.
   (c) manager.

2. The smell of the oil now is
   (a) fuel.
   (b) sweet.
   (c) strong.

3. When the waitress took a sniff of the passing bus, she
   (a) called it.
   (b) touched it.
   (c) smelled it.

4. The story is mainly about
   (a) a waitress who worked for a bus company.
   (b) a bus company that cleaned up a bad smell.
   (c) a rider who passed out.

5. Another title that would best explain the main idea of this story is
   (a) City Buses
   (b) Baby Powder
   (c) Better-Smelling Buses

FIND THE MISSING WORD

In your notebook, complete the following sentences with words from the story. You may look back at the story.

1. Bus riders .... of the strong smell of bus oil.
2. Our buses will smell sweet like baby ....
3. It was put into the .... of 228 buses.
4. "It smells like a bus with .... on, honey," said a waitress.
5. The .... of the bus company said that the buses will smell better.

FIRST THINGS FIRST

Arrange these events in the order in which they really happened.

1. A waitress said that a bus smelled like perfume.
2. Nobody believed the manager.
3. The bus company put Malabate into the fuel tanks of its buses.
4. Car drivers and bus drivers complained about the smell from the buses.
5. The manager said he had an answer to the problem.

IMPROVING YOUR VOCABULARY

Fill in the blank space in each sentence with the word from Column B that best fits. Use each word in Column B only once.

A	B
1. Jose told the .... what we wanted to eat.	(a) gas
2. We stopped to put .... in the car.	(b) manager
3. Willa .... that the teacher gave too much work.	(c) perfume
4. I took a sniff of the .... my mother bought.	(d) complained
5. The .... of our team put Sammy in to pitch.	(e) waitress

---

WORD BUILDING

Alphabetical Order

A. Put these words in alphabetical order.

strong	oil
sniff	man
riders	smash
mad	smell
said	waitress

B. The first letter of all these words is the same. How do you put them in order? Use the *next letter* in each word. The first word is *say*.

slow	smash
skin	shinny
say	

C. The first two letters of all these words is the same. How do you put them in order? Use *the next letter* in each word. The first word is *mad*.

many	make
mash	man
mad	

D. Put these words in alphabetical order.

drivers	baby
fuel	company
perfume	bus
bad	shinny
because	manager

EXPRESSING YOURSELF

1. What ideas do you have for making the city a better place in which to live?

2. Take a whiff. It's the smell of a crowded subway train. What three other city smells can you remember?

3. Write a paragraph using one of these as your first sentence:

(a) That was a bus ride to remember.

(b) If I were mayor of this city, there is one thing I'd do.

(c) There's one smell I love.

(d) There's one smell I can't stand.

3. DANCING FOR RAIN

SCIENTISTS HAVE TRIED TO MAKE RAIN BY SEEDING THE CLOUDS

WHAT DO YOU THINK OF THE WAY THESE FARMERS TRIED TO MAKE RAIN?

HANSKA, Minn. (AP) – It was a hot *July*. There had been no rain for many weeks and the farmers needed rain. They were *worried* that their *crops* might *die*.

About *fifty* farmers put on Indian clothes. Then they did an Indian rain-dance. They hoped the dance would bring rain.

Two of the dancers were sure they would get rain. They were so sure, they *wore* raincoats.

The next day there was a *thunderstorm*. Two *inches* of rain fell on the *dry* farmland.

Some people wondered. Did the rain-dance *cause* the rain?

ST. PETERSBURG (FLORIDA) TIMES

CHECK YOUR UNDERSTANDING

1. The farmers were worried because
  (a) their crops might die.
  (b) it was July.
  (c) they didn't know how to dance.

2. The farmers danced because
  (a) they were Indians.
  (b) they were happy.
  (c) they hoped the dance would bring rain.

3. It rained
  (a) while the farmers danced.
  (b) the same day as the dance.
  (c) the day after the dance.

4. Two dancers wore raincoats because
  (a) it was cold.
  (b) they were sure it would rain.
  (c) it was part of the dance.

5. Another title that would best explain the main idea of this story is:
  (a) Farmers' Rain-Dance Followed by Rain
  (b) Indians in Minnesota
  (c) Dancing for Fun in the City

FIND THE MISSING WORD

In your notebook, complete the following sentences with words from the story. You may look back at the story.

1. The farmers were worried that their . . . . might die.

2. About .... farmers put on Indian clothes.
3. The next day there was a ....
4. Two inches of rain fell on the .... farmland.
5. Did the rain-dance .... the rain?

FIRST THINGS FIRST

Arrange these events in the order in which they really happened.

1. The farmers did a rain-dance.
2. Fifty farmers put on Indian clothes.
3. There was a thunderstorm.
4. It hadn't rained for many weeks.
5. People wondered if the rain-dance caused the rain.

IMPROVING YOUR VOCABULARY

Fill in the blank space in each sentence with the word from Column B that best fits. Use each word in Column B only once.

A	B
1. There are 12 .... in a foot.	(a) dry
2. The teacher wanted to know the .... of Pedro's lateness.	(b) cause
3. After the rain, it took an hour for our clothes to	(c) inches
4. The month that comes after June is	(d) wore
5. Betty .... a new dress to the party.	(e) July

WORD BUILDING

Alphabetical Order

Put these words in alphabetical order.

inches	raincoats
thunderstorm	hoped
work	would
worried	sure
Indian	wonderful

Compound Words

Compound words are made up of two or more words. *Baseball* is a compound word. It is made up of two words: *Base* and *ball.*

Divide each of the following compound words into the separate words that make it up. The first one is done for you.

1. inside *in side*	**6.** thunderstorm
2. nobody	**7.** overcoat
3. raincoat	**8.** nowhere
4. outside	**9.** nearby
5. farmland	**10.** underground

EXPRESSING YOURSELF

1. Either the rain dance caused the rain or it had nothing to do with the rain. What do you believe? Write what you think in three or four sentences.

2. Suppose the farmers do their rain dance next July and it doesn't rain. What would they say about that?

3. Do you believe that you can *make* things happen through magic or will power? Explain.

4. THE STOLEN CAR

STEALING IS WRONG

WAS THE MAN IN THE STORY WRONG
TO STEAL THE CAR?

CANTON, Ohio (AP) – One morning at the *police* station, Policeman Ed Redding *received* a call. The caller said he had just *stolen* a car.

"Is that so? How come?" Redding asked.

"Well," said the man, "I'm taking a walk. I see this car. Its *motor* is running and *nobody* is in it. I thought that any *fool* that leaves his car on the street like that *deserves* to have it stolen. So I stole it."

The man told Redding where he had left the car. He told the policeman that the keys were in a nearby telephone *booth*. Policemen went to *check* if the man had told the *truth*. They found the car and keys where the man said they would be.

—DENVER POST

CHECK YOUR UNDERSTANDING

1. The caller told Ed Redding
  (a) he had just stolen a car.
  (b) Redding's car had been stolen.
  (c) a car was in a telephone booth.

2. The car that was stolen
  (a) had two people in it.
  (b) was never found.
  (c) had its motor running.

3. Police found
  (a) the car and the keys.
  (b) the car, but not the keys.
  (c) the keys, but not the car.

4. "Is that so? How come?" was said by
  (a) the caller.
  (b) Ed Redding.
  (c) the man whose car had been stolen.

5. Another title that would best explain the main idea of this story is:
  (a) A Car in the Street
  (b) The Work of the Police
  (c) A Car Is Stolen To Teach a Lesson

FIND THE MISSING WORD

In your notebook, complete the following sentences with words from the story. You may look at the story.

1. Policeman Ed Redding .... a call.

2. The caller said he had just .... a car.

3. The motor is running and .... is in it.

4. The keys were in a nearby telephone . . . .

5. Police went out to check if the man had told the . . . .

FIRST THINGS FIRST

Arrange these events in the order in which they really happened.

1. The caller said he had stolen a car.
2. Policemen went out to check if the caller had told the truth.
3. The police found the car and the keys.
4. Policeman Ed Redding received a call.
5. The caller told Redding where he had left the car.

IMPROVING YOUR VOCABULARY

Fill in the blank space in each sentence with the word from Column B that best fits. Use each word in Column B only once.

A	B
1. Eric . . . . a bike for his birthday.	(a) motor
2. The driver left the . . . . running.	(b) truth
3. When Joe came in there was . . . . in the house.	(c) received
4. I did not think Chuck was telling the	(d) nobody
5. The car that had been . . . . was found by the police.	(e) stolen

WORD BUILDING

Vowel Sounds

The vowels are *a, e, i, o, u,* and sometimes *y*. They have short sounds and long sounds when you say them.
The *a* in *hat* has a short sound.
The *a* in *hate* has a long sound.

Is the *a* in these five words short or long?

1. and
2. base
3. man
4. that
5. way

Show whether the *a* in each of these words has a short or long vowel sound. Use *ă* if the vowel has a short sound (*hăt*). Use *ā* if the vowel has a long sound (*hāte*). The first one is given as an example.

1. at *ăt*
2. dance
3. station
4. make
5. ask
6. rain
7. day
8. land
9. had
10. way

EXPRESSING YOURSELF

1. Make believe that you are a policeman who has just stopped the driver of the stolen car. Act out what you would say after listening to his story. Get a friend to play the part of the driver.
2. In some neighborhoods the police are kept busy trying to find cars which are stolen by teenagers. Tell why young people commit that kind of crime.
3. The man who stole the car taught a lesson to the car owner. Tell how you would teach a lesson to one of the following:
   (a) a child who never picks up his toys
   (b) a girl who always flirts with her friends' boy friends
   (c) a boy who always picks fights with smaller boys
4. Write a few sentences telling whether you think the man did the right thing in stealing the car. Give your reasons.

5. ORANGE PEOPLE

"AN APPLE A DAY KEEPS THE DOCTOR AWAY"

BUT WHY MIGHT EATING TOO MUCH OF SOME FOODS BRING THE DOCTOR?

Orange people? People the color of the orange you eat?

A *doctor* told of a man who had come to him for help. The man had been living in Alaska for three years. He thought he was not getting enough sunlight there. He ate about four *carrots* a day. He *drank* a large can of *tomato juice* every three days. He *also* ate lots of yellow *vegetables.*

Too many carrots, tomatoes and yellow vegetables caused him to turn orange.

The *cure* was *simple.* The doctor told the man to stop eating all that yellow, orange and red-colored food. The man from Alaska soon turned back to his *original* color.

—SCIENCE NEWS

CHECK YOUR UNDERSTANDING

1. The man who went to see the doctor had been living in
   (a) Alaska.
   (b) Florida.
   (c) California.
2. The man went to see the doctor because
   (a) he was not getting enough sunlight.
   (b) he had turned an orange color.
   (c) he needed more food.
3. The man had turned orange because
   (a) all people living in Alaska turn orange.
   (b) he had stopped eating carrots, tomatoes, and yellow vegetables.
   (c) he ate too many carrots, tomatoes, and yellow vegetables.
4. The man from Alaska
   (a) stayed orange all his life.
   (b) was cured by the doctor.
   (c) was a doctor.
5. Another title that would best explain the main idea of this story is:
   (a) Oranges We Eat
   (b) Doctors and Their Cures
   (c) A Man Who Turned Orange

FIND THE MISSING WORD

In your notebook, complete the following sentences with words from the story. You may look back at the story.

1. A .... told of a man who had come to him for help.
2. The man ate lots of yellow ....

3. Too many carrots, tomatoes, and yellow vegetables .... him to turn orange.
4. The cure was ....
5. The man from Alaska soon turned back to his .... color.

FIRST THINGS FIRST

Arrange these events in the order in which they really happened.

1. The man thought he was not getting enough sunlight in Alaska.
2. The man turned orange.
3. The man turned from orange to his original color.
4. The man moved to Alaska.
5. The man went to see the doctor.

IMPROVING YOUR VOCABULARY

Fill in the blank space in each sentence with the word from Column B that best fits. Use each word in Column B only once.

A	B
1. Anna .... a glass of juice.	(a) carrots
2. Tomatoes are red, but .... are orange.	(b) simple
3. They called the .... when the child got sick.	(c) cure
4. The test was a .... one, and everyone got 100%.	(d) drank
5. We have not yet found a .... for the cold.	(e) doctor

WORD BUILDING

Vowel Sounds

A. Fill in the missing words. You may look back at the vowel exercise in the last story.

1. The vowels are ....
2. The vowels have different sounds. They have .... sounds and .... sounds.
3. The vowel in the word *hat* has a short sound. We put a little mark over the vowel to show it has a short sound. The mark is ....
4. The vowel in the word *hate* has a long sound. We put a little mark over the vowel to show it has a long sound. The mark is ....

The *e* in *set* is short (*sĕt*). The *e* in *me* is long (*mē*).

B. Is the *e* in these words short or long?

1. went
2. we
3. yellow
4. left
5. she

C. Show whether the *e* in each of these words has a short or long vowel sound. Use *ĕ* if the vowel has a short sound (*sĕt*). Use *ē* if the vowel has a long sound (*mē*).

1. well
2. keys
3. red
4. three
5. eat
6. check

7. yellow
8. people
9. Ed
10. left

EXPRESSING YOURSELF

1. The Orange Man was certainly "different." Tell about someone you know who is "different" —in the way he looks, the way he acts, or the way he thinks.
2. The man from Alaska had a strange diet. Tell about someone you know who has strange eating habits.
3. Write a few sentences telling how you would feel if you found your skin color turning orange –or green.

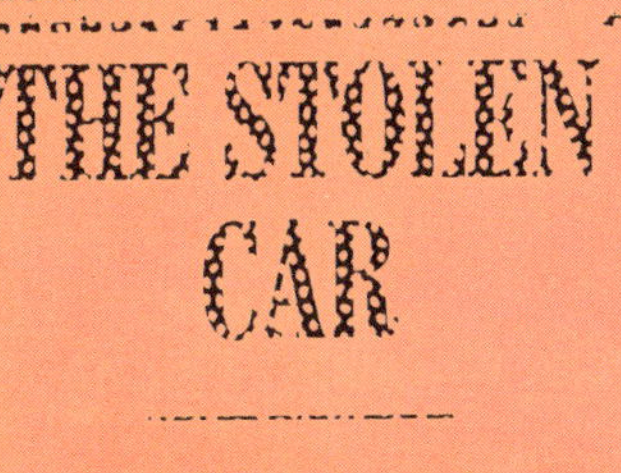

REVIEW OF LESSONS 1-5

FINDING THE MISSING WORD

The sentences below are followed by a list of *italicized* words. For each sentence, write the word that fits best in the blank. Use each word only once. (The number in parentheses tells you the number of the story in which the word was first used.)

1. James cut down the .... coconut from the tree.
2. Rod's .... became red from lying in the hot sun.
3. The toy cost .... cents.
4. The ruler was 12 .... long.
5. The .... caught the bank robber.
6. We went in to .... if Frank was still there.

7. Sid went outside and found that his car had been ....
8. It was so hot, we .... one soda after another.
9. Anne has orange .... for breakfast every morning.
10. A .... came after two weeks without rain.

(a) *fifty* (3)
(b) *police* (4)
(c) *stolen* (4)
(d) *thunderstorm* (3)
(e) *ripest* (1)
(f) *check* (4)
(g) *juice* (5)
(h) *drank* (5)
(i) *inches* (3)
(j) *skin* (1)

FINDING THE OPPOSITE

For each of the *italicized* words, choose the word on the right that is most nearly opposite. (The number in parentheses tells you the number of the story in which the word was first used.)

1. *cure* (5) — (a) goodness; (b) fairness; (c) illness
2. *cool* (1) — (a) warm; (b) cold; (c) soda
3. *die* (3) — (a) live; (b) change; (c) try
4. *stolen* (4) — (a) gone; (b) returned; (c) forgotten
5. *dry* (3) — (a) hot; (b) wet; (c) soft
6. *loose* (1) — (a) tight; (b) extra; (c) better
7. *nobody* (4) — (a) health; (b) forward; (c) everybody
8. *received* (4) — (a) fell; (b) knew; (c) gave
9. *simple* (5) — (a) true; (b) hard; (c) new
10. *truth* (4) — (a) talk; (b) mouth; (c) lie

UNSCRAMBLING THE WORD

Each of the definitions below is followed by a scrambled word that fits the meaning. Unscramble the letters to find the word. (The number in parentheses tells you the number of the story in which the word was first used.)

1.	a small closed place for a telephone (4)	OBHTO
2.	orange-colored vegetable (5)	TCAROR
3.	anything that can be burned to make heat or power (2)	EFLU
4.	something put into automobiles to make them run (2)	SAG
5.	the seventh month (3)	LJYU
6.	the person who runs a business (2)	AGMRAEN
7.	kind of tree that grows in warm places (1)	MAPL
8.	something with a sweet smell (2)	EMPEFRU
9.	to smell (2)	FINSF
10.	juicy, round, red fruit used as a vegetable (5)	TOOTAM

FINDING THE RIGHT MEANING

For each of the *italicized* words, choose its correct meaning from the choices on the right. (The number in parentheses tells you the number of the story in which the word was first used.)

1. *cause* (3) (a) person, thing, or event that makes something happen; (b) center of something; (c) hardest part of a lesson

2. *complain* (2) (a) to say that something is wrong; (b) to tell how something works; (c) to try to do better

3. *crops* (3) (a) things which everyone says are true; (b) policemen; (c) plants grown by people for food or other uses

4. *cure* (5) (a) to make well; (b) to say hard words to; (c) to play

5. *deserve* (4) (a) to keep away from; (b) to try hard; (c) to have a right to

6. *fool* (4) (a) last person in a room; (b) person without sense; (c) something used to make an automobile go

7. *motor* (4) (a) part of the machine that makes it go; (b) person who helps others; (c) something used to tell how fast an automobile is going

8. *thirsty* (1) (a) having 30 parts; (b) wanting to drink; (c) saving money

9. *wore* (3) (a) fought hard; (b) had on the body; (c) happened

10. *worried* (3) (a) tired; (b) relaxed; (c) uneasy

6. ASK ANN

A GIRL GETS STOMACH PAINS BEFORE EVERY DATE

WHAT ADVICE WOULD YOU GIVE HER?

DEAR ANN: I am nearly 17 and have had this *problem* for over a year.

Whenever I am asked for a *date,* I get real excited about it. I look *forward* so much to having a good time. So what happens? About ten minutes before my date shows up, I get *stomach pains.* By the time he *arrives* I feel terrible.

I have these pains the *whole* evening. It's all I can do to *force* a smile and make believe I'm having fun. It kills me to see other girls laughing and having a good time while I'm in pain——wishing I was *dead.*

Please tell me how to get over this. I am —*Sick* of Getting Sick.

—LANCASTER (PENNSYLVANIA) NEW ERA

CHECK YOUR UNDERSTANDING

1. The girl who wrote the letter
(a) does not like to go out on dates.
(b) would like to kill other girls.
(c) gets stomach pains before a date.

2. Her stomach pains
(a) go away after a few minutes.
(b) start days before her date.
(c) last the whole evening of the date.

3. On her date, the girl
(a) forces a smile.
(b) tells everyone she does not feel well.
(c) laughs and really has a good time.

4. The girl wrote Ann
(a) to tell other girls not to go out on dates.
(b) to ask for help.
(c) to help Ann.

5. Another title that would best explain the main idea of this letter is:
(a) A Girl Feels Terrible About Pains on Dates
(b) The Problem of Being 17
(c) Making Believe Can Bring Good Times

FIND THE MISSING WORD

In your notebook, complete the following sentences with words from the story. You may look back at the story.

1. I look .... to having a good time.

2. About ten minutes before my date shows up, I get .... pains.

3. By the time he .... I feel terrible.
4. I have these pains the .... evening.
5. It's all I can do to .... a smile.

FIRST THINGS FIRST

Arrange these events in the order in which they really happened to the girl who wrote the letter to Ann.

1. She had stomach pains all evening.
2. She wrote a letter to Ann.
3. She was asked for a date.
4. She felt terrible when the date arrived.
5. She began getting stomach pains ten minutes before the date showed up.

IMPROVING YOUR VOCABULARY

Pick out the word from Column B which is the opposite of the word in Column A.

A	B
1. arrives	(a) well
2. dead	(b) part
3. forward	(c) back
4. sick	(d) leaves
5. whole	(e) alive

WORD BUILDING

Vowel Sounds

A. Is the vowel sound long or short in each of

these words? If it is short, put ˘ over the italicized vowel. If it is long, put ‒ over the italicized vowel. Use this key if you need it.

hăt hāte
sĕt mē

1. d*a*te
2. *a*m
3. m*a*ke
4. h*a*ppen
5. h*a*d
6. *E*d
7. l*e*ft
8. f*e*el
9. sh*e*
10. w*e*ek

The *i* in *hid* is short (*hĭd*). The *i* in *child* is long (*chīld*).

B. Is the *i* in these words *short* or *long*?
1. it
2. while
3. sick
4. light
5. this

C. Show whether the *i* in each of these words has a short or long vowel sound. Use *ĭ* if the vowel has a short sound (*hĭd*). Use *ī* if the vowel has a long sound (*chīld*).
1. I
2. wish
3. excited
4. five
5. smile
6. his

7. mind
8. right
9. simple
10. in

EXPRESSING YOURSELF

1. Here is Ann's answer to the letter:

   Dear Sick of Getting Sick: Go to a doctor and learn whether or not a stomach problem is causing the pain. Chances are good that the trouble is not in your stomach but higher up—like in your head.

   People who are uptight often develop pains. Stomach aches and headaches are the most common. Hopefully the doctor will give you some medicine or suggest counseling. Maybe both.

   Would your advice to the young lady who gets sick before every date be the same as Ann's? How would it be different?
2. Is there anything that gets you nervous? What can you do to get rid of your nervousness?
3. Many people write to newspapers about their problems, hoping to get answers to whatever is troubling them. Take a real problem which you have, or one which you have made up, and write a short letter in which you "Ask Ann" for advice.

7. DON'T SMOKE, JOE

MOST DOCTORS WILL TELL YOU CIGARETTE SMOKING IS A BAD HABIT

HOW CAN YOU HELP A FRIEND WHO WANTS TO END THIS BAD HABIT?

PASSAIC, N.J. (AP) – Fire *Captain* Joe Stone has friends all over town. These friends are all trying to get him to stop *smoking*.

They have put up signs saying, "Don't Smoke, Joe." These signs look down at Joe any place he might go to *sneak* a smoke.

Ads in the city *newspaper* tell him: "Don't Smoke, Joe."

Joe has *discovered* he can't bum a *cigarette* anywhere in this city of 53,714 people.

It all began when a doctor told him to stop smoking. Joe had been smoking for *thirty* years. It wasn't going to be easy to stop.

To help him, about thirty of his friends gave money to buy the newspaper ad. A fireman who could *draw* well made the signs.

Joe's friends made up their *minds* Joe will stop. They will do anything to see that he does not smoke.

—MILWAUKEE JOURNAL

CHECK YOUR UNDERSTANDING

1. Joe Stone has
   (a) many friends.
   (b) no friends.
   (c) two or three friends.

2. Joe Stone's friends
   (a) want him to smoke.
   (b) help him to sneak a smoke.
   (c) want him to stop smoking.

3. Joe Stone
   (a) has been smoking for thirty years.
   (b) is a doctor.
   (c) took an ad in a newspaper.

4. Joe Stone sees, "Don't Smoke, Joe,"
   (a) on signs, but not in newspapers.
   (b) in newspapers, but not on signs.
   (c) on signs and in newspapers.

5. Another title that would best explain the main idea of this story is:
   (a) Joe's Life As a Fire Captain
   (b) The Ad in the Newspaper
   (c) Friends Don't Let Joe Smoke

FIND THE MISSING WORD

In your notebook, complete the following sentences with words from the story. You may look back at the story.

1. Joe Stone's friends are all trying to get him to stop ....
2. Ads in the city .... tell him: "Don't Smoke, Joe."
3. Joe has discovered he can't bum a .... anywhere.
4. A fireman who could .... well made the signs.
5. They have made up their .... Joe will stop.

PROBABLY . . .

Choose the answer most likely to be true.

1. Joe Stone's friends
   (a) don't like him at all.
   (b) don't care what he does.
   (c) like him very much.
2. Joe Stone's friends think
   (a) Joe would never try to smoke again.
   (b) Joe would still try to smoke.
   (c) smoking is good for him.
3. The doctor told Joe to stop smoking because
   (a) the doctor didn't smoke.
   (b) Joe might die if he didn't stop smoking.
   (c) the smoke got in the doctor's eyes.
4. Thirty friends gave the money to buy the newspaper ad because
   (a) the newspaper said that all thirty had to pay.

(b) Joe made them do it.
(c) the ad cost too much for just one friend to pay for.

IMPROVING YOUR VOCABULARY

Fill in the blank space in each sentence with the word from Column B that best fits. Use each word in Column B only once.

A	B
1. I read all about the fire in the	(a) captain
2. The best player was made . . . . of the team.	(b) cigarette
3. Matt . . . . he had left his English book at home.	(c) newspaper
4. Ella was smoking a	(d) thirty
5. There are . . . . days in the month of June.	(e) discovered

---

WORD BUILDING

Vowel Sounds

A. Is the italicized vowel sound long or short in each of these words? If it is short, put ˘ over the vowel. If it is long, put – over the vowel. Use this key if you need it.

hăt	hāte
sĕt	mē
hĭd	chīld

1. *a*sk
2. aw*a*y
3. *A*nn
4. sh*e*
5. g*e*ts
6. f*ee*l
7. th*i*s
8. *i*t
9. m*i*nd
10. adv*i*ce

B. The *o* in *hot* is short (*hŏt*). The *o* in *go* is long (*gō*). Is the *o* in these words short or long?

1. stone
2. stop
3. clothes
4. Joe
5. got

C. Show whether the *o* in each of these words has a short or long vowel sound. Use *ŏ* if the vowel has a short sound (*hŏt*). Use *ō* if the vowel has a long sound (*gō*).

1. smoke
2. over
3. no
4. told
5. stole
6. lots
7. hoped
8. got
9. stop
10. hotel

EXPRESSING YOURSELF

1. Do you think that Joe Stone's friends are doing the right thing, or should they mind their own business? Why?
2. Make believe that you are a friend of Joe's who wants him to stop smoking. Make up a newspaper ad (with drawings) which will show him that smoking is bad for his health.
3. In the last few years there has been no cigarette advertising allowed on television. Tell why you think that has (or has not) cut down on cigarette smoking in this country.
4. Write a few sentences about a good friend. Be sure to tell what your friend has done to prove his friendship for you.
5. Write a few sentences telling whether or not you think smoking cigarettes is dangerous to health. Ask your school librarian to help you find information on cigarette smoking and its effect on health.

8. YOUTHS CLEAN CREEKS

OUR WATER IS DIRTY,
OUR AIR IS BAD TO BREATHE,
OUR LAND IS FULL OF LITTER

WHAT CAN WE DO TO HELP?

ATLANTA, Ga. – What do these things have in *common?*

1. two television sets
2. a *refrigerator*
3. parts for a truck
4. a pair of glasses
5. a *toilet* seat
6. lots of *beer* cans
7. the bones of a dead dog

Give up? They were all pulled out of two *creeks* Friday. 75 *students* from Atlanta high schools used a day off from school to clean out Peavine Creek and Peachtree Creek. They did this because they are *interested* in ecology*.

"We pulled out all sorts of *junk,*" said Ken Kohler, a student at one of the schools. They had worked on cleaning the creeks three weeks ago. "But there was so much junk we had to go back," Kohler said.

He added that some people had gotten together to keep the creeks clean. "But it's a losing *battle.* People just go over there and *dump* stuff in as fast as we can pull it out.

"It's pretty sad," he said.

—ATLANTA CONSTITUTION

* ecology – the study of the relationship between living things and their environment.

CHECK YOUR UNDERSTANDING

1. On their day off from school, the 75 students
   (a) bought two television sets and a refrigerator.
   (b) cleaned out two creeks.
   (c) dumped junk into two creeks.

2. The students
   (a) had cleaned the creeks 3 weeks ago.
   (b) wanted to make some money.
   (c) were made to clean the creeks by their teachers.

3. Ken Kohler
   (a) thinks they can keep the creeks clean.
   (b) is happy about the way the creeks are.
   (c) is a student in an Atlanta high school.

4. Which of these was *not* pulled from the creek by the students?
   (a) parts for a truck.
   (b) a set of dishes.
   (c) a pair of glasses.

5. Another title that would best explain the main idea of this story is:
   (a) A Day Off From School
   (b) Two Creeks in Georgia
   (c) The Creeks That Can't Be Kept Clean

FIND THE MISSING WORD

In your notebook, complete the following sentences with words from the story. You may look back at the story.

1. . . . . from Atlanta high schools cleaned out two creeks.

2. The students are . . . . in ecology.

3. People . . . . stuff in the creeks as fast as the students can pull it out.

4. The students pulled out all sorts of . . . .

5. Kohler said, "It's a losing . . . ."

WHAT'S THE REASON?

When you read you sometimes have to be a good detective. You have to find out *why* things happen. See if you can find the right "why" in these answers.

1. The students cleaned the creeks because
   (a) they were interested in ecology.
   (b) it was part of their general science class lesson.

(c) they had nothing else to do on their day off.

2. The students cleaned the creeks for the second time because
   (a) it was a lot of fun the first time.
   (b) there were many things there that they could sell.
   (c) there was too much junk to clean out the first time.
3. There was so much junk in the creeks because
   (a) the students are interested in ecology.
   (b) most people don't care about keeping the creeks clean.
   (c) a truck turned over and dumped its things into the creek.
4. Ken Kohler said, "It's a losing battle" because
   (a) there aren't enough interested students.
   (b) the school won't give any more days off.
   (c) people dump stuff in the creeks as fast as the students can pull it out.

IMPROVING YOUR VOCABULARY

Fill in the blank space in each sentence with the word from Column B that best fits. Use each word in Column B only once.

A	B
1. There are 3,000 .... in our school.	(a) interested (b) refrigerator
2. Luis was very .... in the story Maria was telling.	(c) dump (d) students (e) battle

3. The brothers had a .... over which program to watch on TV.
4. Since she was hungry, she went to the ....
5. People would .... junk in the creeks.

WORD BUILDING

Vowel Sounds

A. Is the sound of the italicized vowel long or short in each of these words? If it is short, put ˘ over the vowel. If it is long, put ‒ over the vowel. Use this key if you need it.

hăt	hāte
sĕt	mē
hĭd	chīld
hŏt	gō

1. *a*ges
2. gl*a*ss
3. tw*e*lve
4. f*e*ll
5. d*i*ed
6. sk*i*n
7. wh*i*te
8. y*e*ll*o*w
9. n*o*
10. sh*o*p

The *u* in *but* is short (*bŭt*). The *u* in *cute* is long (*cūte*).

B. Is the *u* in these words short or long?

1. truck
2. dump
3. junk
4. juice
5. but

C. Show whether the *u* in each of these words has a short or long vowel sound. Use *ŭ* if the vowel has a short sound (*cŭt*). Use *ū* if the vowel has a long sound (*cūte*).

1. used	**6.** bus
2. dunk	**7.** perfume
3. use	**8.** sunlight
4. much	**9.** fuel
5. fun	**10.** sudden

EXPRESSING YOURSELF

1. Make a list of three places in your neighborhood which need a clean-up job like the one in this story. Try to find out who is supposed to keep those places clean.
2. Suppose you wanted a few of your friends to help you clean up the school's lunchroom or athletic field. Make up a sign with a saying (like "Clean is Beautiful") which you could post in the hallway.
3. We often hear older people saying that young people today are "no good." In a few sentences write about a young person or young people you know who did something to help others.
4. Visit an empty lot in your neighborhood. Make a list of the junk you see there.

9. YOUNG, BUT OLD

HOW OLD IS OLD?

CAN A PERSON BE OLD AT 12?

VITORIA, Brazil, Jan. 28–A 12-year-old boy died today of old *age*. Jomar Silva of Brazil was only 12, but his *body* was that of a 90-year-old man.

At six *months,* Jomar's *teeth* were *crooked* and yellow.

His hair started turning white and fell out before he was two.

At 10, his skin was dry and *wrinkled*. His *blood vessels* began to get hard.

His doctors said that Jomar had a *disease* that hits one man in a *million*. Someone who has this disease ages about eight years for every one that he lives.

—ST. LOUIS POST-DISPATCH

CHECK YOUR UNDERSTANDING

1. Jomar Silva died at the age of
(a) 90.
(b) 28.
(c) 12.

2. At six months, Jomar's
(a) skin was dry and wrinkled.
(b) hair started turning white.
(c) teeth were crooked and yellow.

3. Before he was two years old, Jomar's
(a) blood vessels began to get hard.
(b) hair fell out.
(c) skin was wrinkled.

4. Jomar died from a disease that
(a) many people have.
(b) hits one man in a million.
(c) he got at the age of 90.

5. Another title that would best explain the main idea of this story is:
(a) A Boy from Brazil
(b) An Old Man Dies at Age 12
(c) Teeth, Hair, and Skin

FIND THE MISSING WORD

In your notebook, complete the following sentences with words from the story. You may look back at the story.

1. His . . . . was that of a 90-year-old man.

2. At six months, Jomar's teeth were . . . . and yellow.

3. At 10, his skin was dry and . . . .

4. His . . . . vessels began to get hard.
5. His doctors said that Jomar had a . . . . that hits one man in a million.

FIRST THINGS FIRST

Arrange these events in the order in which they really happened to Jomar Silva.

1. He died.
2. His hair started turning white.
3. His blood vessels began to get hard.
4. His teeth became crooked and yellow.

IMPROVING YOUR VOCABULARY

Fill in the blank space in each sentence with the word from Column B that best fits. Use each word in Column B only once.

A	B
1. After Pete ate, he discovered that pieces of food were stuck between his	(a) blood
2. The boy said he was ten years of	(b) months
3. It was a deep cut and much . . . . came out.	(c) disease
4. July and August are summer	(d) teeth
5. Chickenpox is a . . . . many children get.	(e) age

WORD BUILDING

Alphabetical Order

Put these words in alphabetical order:

because	cool
cut	fuel
July	Caribbean
cookies	riders
waitress	oil

Compound Words

A. Break up these words into two words:

1. policeman
2. someone
3. inside
4. thunderstorm
5. cannot

B. Put together a word in Column A and a word in Column B to make a compound word. Here is the first one: *near* + *by* = *nearby*.

A	B
1. near	(a) paper
2. sun	(b) land
3. farm	(c) by
4. news	(d) light
5. rain	(e) coat

Vowel Sounds

Each of the italicized words below is followed by three choices. Choose the word having the same vowel sound as the word in italics.

1. *hat*	make	ask	day
2. *set*	keys	be	yellow
3. *hid*	wish	right	smile
4. *hot*	over	stop	smoke
5. *but*	pure	perfume	bus
6. *hate*	rain	dance	land
7. *me*	left	she	check
8. *child*	simple	his	mind
9. *go*	stone	job	lots
10. *cute*	used	junk	fun

EXPRESSING YOURSELF

1. Ask the school doctor or your family doctor to explain what went wrong inside Jomar's body which made him die of old age. Tell your findings to the class. (The disease he died of is called *progeria.* You can find information about it in an encyclopedia.)
2. What if science could let you control your age and you could be any age you wished? Tell what age you would choose to be, and why.
3. Suppose a twelve-year-old boy in your neighborhood died after having been hit by a car. In three or four sentences, write whether you would feel more sorry for him or for Jomar Silva of Brazil.

10. A SHORT HONEYMOON

NOT KNOWING THE MEANING OF WORDS CAN LEAD TO MISUNDERSTANDINGS

WHAT MISTAKE DID THE SOLDIER MAKE
BECAUSE HE DIDN'T KNOW
JE NE SAIS PAS IS FRENCH
AND MEANS **I DON'T KNOW**?

During the *war* a *soldier* from Kentucky was in Paris, France. As he walked along, he passed a *church*. Just then, a *wedding* party came out. He stopped to watch.

The *groom* was not more than five feet tall. The soldier watched as the little groom helped his big bride into a waiting *taxi.*

"What's the little *fellow*'s name?" the soldier asked a nearby policeman.

The French policeman smiled and said, *"Je ne sais pas."*

The soldier kept walking. Some time later he passed the same church. This time a *funeral* was taking place.

"Who died?" the soldier asked the same policeman.

The French policeman smiled. *"Je ne sais pas,"* he said once more.

"I'll be," the soldier said. "Poor little fellow didn't last long, did he?"

—LOUISVILLE COURIER-JOURNAL

CHECK YOUR UNDERSTANDING

1. The wedding took place
  (a) in Germany.
  (b) in Kentucky.
  (c) in France.

2. The soldier
  (a) thought he understood what the policeman said.
  (b) really understood what the policeman said.
  (c) was making fun of the policeman because the policeman couldn't speak English.

3. The groom
  (a) died.
  (b) was a friend of the policeman.
  (c) helped his bride into a waiting taxi.

4. This story is meant
   (a) to be sad.
   (b) to be funny.
   (c) to teach you French.
5. The main idea of this story is:
   (a) Little men shouldn't marry.
   (b) If you don't know a language, you may not understand what someone is saying.
   (c) You should not ask policemen questions.

FIND THE MISSING WORD

In your notebook, complete the following sentences with words from the story. You may look back at the story.

1. A .... from Kentucky was in Paris.
2. The .... was not more than five feet tall.
3. The groom helped his bride into a waiting ....
4. The .... waved to her friends.
5. When the soldier passed the church again, a .... was taking place.

FIRST THINGS FIRST

Arrange these events in the order in which they really happened.

1. A funeral was taking place in the church.
2. The soldier thought the groom had died.
3. A wedding party came out of the church.
4. The soldier asked the policeman the name of the groom.
5. The soldier asked the policeman who had died.

IMPROVING YOUR VOCABULARY

Pick out the word from Column B which is most nearly *opposite* of the word in Column A.

A	B
1. fellow	(a) groom
2. war	(b) divorce
3. bride	(c) girl
4. funeral	(d) birth
5. wedding	(e) peace

WORD BUILDING

Syllables

A syllable is a word or part of a word that is sounded together. Usually, if a word has only one vowel sound, it has only one syllable. If a word has two vowel sounds, it usually has two syllables. If a word has three vowel sounds, it usually has three syllables. For example, *go* has one syllable because you say only one vowel sound—*go*. *Began* has two syllables because you say two vowel sounds—*be gan*. *Understand* has three syllables because you say three vowel sounds—*un der stand*.

Read each of these words. Next to it, write the number of syllables the word has.

1. kept	**6.** student
2. Paris	**7.** together
3. fellow	**8.** common
4. walking	**9.** over
5. last	**10.** Atlanta

body is in it. I thought that any fool that leaves his car on the street like that deserves to have it stolen. So I stole it."

The man told Reg...

THE STOLEN CAR

CANTON, Ohio (AP) — ... morning at the ...

Nine-foot Woman

ALLAHABAD, India, Chronicle Foreign Service—A ...year-old peasant is wandering the streets of Indian towns because no one wants to give her shelter. There are thousands of poor begging in this country, but Rasmanjari Rani is unwa... for a strange reason.

Rasmanjari is nearly nine feet tall—one of the tallest wo... in the world.

When she went to a ... house the other day, the ... locked the door after one ... at her.

"Maybe he thought I was a witch," the dark-eyed wo...

Orange People

REVIEW OF LESSONS 6-10

FINDING THE MISSING WORD

The sentences below are followed by a list of *italicized* words. For each sentence, write the word that fits best in the blank. Use each word only once. (The number in parentheses tells you the number of the story in which the word was first used.)

1. The bus fare was raised to .... cents.
2. The old man had a .... face.
3. Kenny got a job driving a ....
4. Carmen and Tony are having a June ....
5. Joan's .... was that her parents didn't like her boy friend.

. Paul goes to .... every Sunday.

EXPRESSING YOURSELF

1. Tell of a time when you got into trouble because you did not understand the meaning of some word or words.
2. Have your teacher write a message of 10-20 words on a slip of paper. The message might be something like this: "On November 18 there will be no school because of a teachers' meeting." Then, have your teacher *tell* the message to the student in the first row, first seat. That student will tell the message to the student behind him, and so on—around the class. When the message has gone through the entire class, let the last student tell the class the message. Compare it to the one written on the paper. Was there misunderstanding? If so, why do you think there was?
3. Write a few sentences telling why you, as a girl, would or would not marry someone shorter than you. If you are a boy, write why you would or would not marry a girl taller than you.

7. We put the soda into the .... to keep it cold.
8. There was a "No ...." sign on the bus.
9. Over eight .... people live in New York City.
10. Sue had a .... for eight o'clock that night.

(a) *wrinkled* (9)
(b) *wedding* (10)
(c) *refrigerator* (8)
(d) *million* (9)
(e) *date* (6)
(f) *thirty* (7)
(g) *smoking* (7)
(h) *taxi* (10)
(i) *problem* (6)
(j) *church* (10)

FINDING THE OPPOSITE

For each of the *italicized* words, choose the word on the right that is most nearly opposite. (The number in parentheses tells you the number of the story in which the word was first used.)

1. *arrives* (6) — (a) tells; (b) receives; (c) leaves
2. *bride* (10) — (a) wedding; (b) groom; (c) broom
3. *crooked* (9) — (a) straight; (b) lost; (c) cool
4. *discovered* (7) — (a) lost; (b) spent; (c) found
5. *fellow* (10) — (a) adult; (b) girl; (c) captain
6. *forward* (6) — (a) backward; (b) upward; (c) downward
7. *sick* (6) — (a) cold; (b) easy; (c) well

8. *student* (8) (a) school; (b) teacher; (c) patient
9. *war* (10) (a) peace; (b) truth; (c) battle
10. *whole* (6) (a) better; (b) simple; (c) part

UNSCRAMBLING THE WORD

Each of the definitions below is followed by a scrambled word that fits the meaning. Unscramble the letters to find the word. (The number in parentheses tells you the number of the story in which the word was first used.)

1.	belonging equally to all (8)	MNOCMO
2.	to make a picture of (7)	WARD
3.	wanting to know about something (8)	TSTNIRDEEE
4.	something that is worthless (8)	UKJN
5.	one of twelve periods of time into which a year is divided (9)	NMHTO
6.	the part of a person that knows and thinks (7)	NMDI
7.	sheets of printed paper containing the news (7)	PNEREPWAS
8.	to act like a person who is ashamed to be seen (7)	AESKN
9.	part of the body which receives eaten food (6)	HTSCMOA
10.	part of the mouth used for biting and chewing (9)	HTETE

FINDING THE RIGHT MEANING

For each of the *italicized* words, choose its correct meaning from the choices on the right. (The number in parentheses tells you the number of the story in which the word was first used.)

1. *age* (9)	(a) the first time; (b) ill health; (c) time of life
2. *battle* (8)	(a) fight; (b) cover; (c) cure
3. *captain* (7)	(a) follower; (b) leader; (c) man
4. *creek* (8)	(a) squeaky sound; (b) big door; (c) small stream
5. *disease* (9)	(a) health; (b) sickness; (c) doctor
6. *dump* (8)	(a) to throw out; (b) to get back; (c) to turn down
7. *during* (10)	(a) through the whole time of; (b) before the last time; (c) after the first time
8. *force* (6)	(a) to say that something is wrong; (b) to find what one is looking for; (c) to make one act against his will
9. *pains* (6)	(a) sharp objects; (b) things one hopes to do; (c) feelings of hurt
10. *soldier* (10)	(a) man who serves in the airforce; (b) man who serves in the army; (c) man who serves in the navy

11. WAS IT WORTH IT?

YOU SEE A GROUP OF BOYS BEATING UP ANOTHER BOY

WHAT DO YOU DO?

One night Mike Collins was with his girl. They were *having* something to eat at a roadside stand.

Suddenly they heard a lot of noise outside in the parking lot. Mike went to see what was happening. He saw a boy *lying* on the ground. A *group* of older boys were *beating* him.

Mike stepped in to help the boy on the ground. There were ten of the others. The last thing Mike remembers is that someone hit him in the face with something *metal.*

At the *hospital,* they found Mike's face had been broken in three places. Six weeks later, Mike came home. He will need an *operation* on his eye. He had been working in the day and going to *college* at night. Now he cannot go to work or to school.

Not one of the ten boys has been *arrested.* No one has been able to say who the boy was who hit Mike with the metal.

Was it *worth* it for Mike?

—NEWSDAY (LONG ISLAND, N.Y.)

CHECK YOUR UNDERSTANDING

1. Mike Collins and his girl were
  (a) eating.
  (b) standing.
  (c) driving along.

2. When Mike went out to the parking lot, he saw
  (a) some boys singing.
  (b) a boy lying on the ground.
  (c) two boys having a fight.

3. When Mike tried to help the boy who was being beaten, he
  (a) drove the other boys off.
  (b) got beaten up himself.
  (c) got hit by the boy he was trying to help.

4. Now, Mike
  (a) is back at school.
  (b) needs an operation on his eye.
  (c) is in jail.

5. This story is mainly about
  (a) a young man who helped a group of boys win a fight.
  (b) eating at a roadside stand.
  (c) a young man who got hurt trying to help a boy in a fight.

FIND THE MISSING WORD

In your notebook, complete the following sentences with words from the story. You may look back at the story.

1. Mike saw a boy . . . . on the ground.

2. Someone hit Mike in the face with something made of . . . .

3. Mike will need an .... on his eye.
4. Mike had been going to .... at night.
5. Not one of the ten boys has been ....

FIRST THINGS FIRST

Arrange these events in the order in which they really happened to Mike Collins.

1. He saw a group of boys beating another boy.
2. He got hit in the face with something made of metal.
3. He and his girl were having something to eat.
4. He went out to the parking lot to see what was happening.
5. He went to the hospital.

IMPROVING YOUR VOCABULARY

Fill in the blank space in each sentence with the word from Column B that best fits. Use each word in Column B only once.

A	B
1. Larry was .... on the ground when we found him.	(a) having
2. A .... of girls was standing by the door.	(b) hospital
3. After high school, many students go on to	(c) lying
4. My uncle had to go to the .... for an operation on his eye.	(d) college
5. We were all .... a good time.	(e) group

WORD BUILDING

Syllables

A. Complete the following sentences. You may look back at the last Word Building exercise.

1. A syllable is a word or part of a word that is .... together.
2. If a word has two vowel sounds, it will usually have two ....
3. The word *began* has .... syllables.

When a consonant is doubled in the middle of a word, the word is divided between the two consonants. For example, *better* is divided into *bet ter.*

B. Divide each of these words into two syllables:

1. wedding
2. fellow
3. common
4. carrot
5. getting

EXPRESSING YOURSELF

1. In this story, Mike Collins was hurt trying to help someone. Tell a story you know of someone who successfully helped a person or persons in trouble.
2. Not one of the ten boys was arrested. Would you go to court and identify one of them if you

had been a witness to the beating? Give reasons for your answer.

3. The last line of this story asks, "Was it worth it for Mike?" In a few sentences, write your answer to that question.

12. ALL'S WELL THAT ENDS WELL

PATRICIA CHANCE WAS ROBBED BY A THIEF BUT HELPED BY HER FRIENDS

WHAT DOES THIS STORY TEACH YOU ABOUT PEOPLE?

Often a bad *dream* can have a happy ending. And that's what happened to a beautiful black girl–Patricia Chance.

Last Saturday evening Patricia was getting ready to take off from Kennedy *Airport*. She was flying to Spain. She had won a *scholarship* to *study* there.

Miss Chance, 21, had spent many hours making her own clothes and saving pennies to buy shoes, books, and other things she needed.

She and a friend stopped a *cab* at the door of her home. They *loaded* the cab with everything she was taking with her. Then they made their *mistake.* They left the cab waiting while they went back upstairs for final goodbyes.

When they returned, the cab was gone. All Miss Chance had left was her air ticket to Spain. Everything else had been stolen by the cab driver.

People in Harlem heard what had happened. Before you knew it, Miss Chance had four new *suitcases,* new clothes, even a new *wig.* People who cared had given the bad dream a happy ending.

—AMSTERDAM (NEW YORK CITY) NEWS

CHECK YOUR UNDERSTANDING

1. Patricia Chance was going to Spain
- (a) to travel.
- (b) to study.
- (c) to work for an airline.

2. Patricia Chance
- (a) was a rich girl.
- (b) made her own clothes.
- (c) is 18 years old.

3. Patricia's mistake was
- (a) flying to Spain.
- (b) winning a scholarship.
- (c) leaving everything she owned in the cab.

4. This story shows that
- (a) you can't expect help from anyone.
- (b) all people are good.
- (c) some people are good, some are bad.

5. Another title that would best explain the main idea of this story is:
- (a) From Bad Dream to Happy Ending

(b) Flying to Spain to Study
(c) She Made Her Own Clothes

FIND THE MISSING WORD

In your notebook, complete the following sentences with words from the story. You may look back at the story.

1. She had won a .... and was going to study in Spain.
2. A bad .... can turn into a story with a happy ending.
3. Patricia was getting ready to take off from Kennedy ....
4. They .... the cab with everything she was taking with her.
5. Miss Chance had four new ....

FIRST THINGS FIRST

Arrange these events in the order in which they really happened to Patricia Chance.

1. She and a friend went upstairs for final goodbyes.
2. People in Harlem came to her help.
3. The cab driver drove away with all her belongings.
4. She won a scholarship.
5. She and a friend loaded the cab with everything she was taking with her.

IMPROVING YOUR VOCABULARY

Fill in the blank space in each sentence with the word from Column B that best fits. Use each word in Column B only once.

A	B
1. We waited at the .... for her plane to come in.	(a) dream
2. I had a .... that there was no more war.	(b) loaded
3. We .... the car with her suitcases.	(c) airport
4. Jimmy comes to my house very	(d) study
5. I will have to .... for my English test.	(e) often

WORD BUILDING

Syllables

A. Divide these words into syllables. If the word has only one syllable, copy it and put a circle around it.

1. yellow
2. getting
3. common
4. what
5. happen

When there are two consonants between two vowels, the word is usually divided between the two consonants. For example, the word *mistake* is divided as *mis take*. In *mistake,* the two consonants that are together are *st*. The consonants *st* are between two vowels *i* and *a*.

You divide the word *mistake* between the two consonants *s* and *t*.

B. Divide each of these words into two syllables:

1. sister
2. person
3. also
4. soldier
5. Harlem

EXPRESSING YOURSELF

1. Tell of a time when something was stolen from you. Also, tell how you felt about it.

2. What is meant by the title, "All's Well That Ends Well"? Tell of something which started out unhappily for you but ended in a better way.

3. Tell about a mistake you made in your opinion of a person.

4. Write a paragraph about one of these:
(a) A Bad Dream
(b) A Happy Ending
(c) Helping Others

13. THE MAN WHO TRIED TO FLY

WE NEED SOMEONE TO PUT ON WINGS AND FLY LIKE A BIRD. WANT TO TRY?

WHY DOES BIG WALTER DO SUCH THINGS?

LONDON, England – Walter Cornelius has a broken nose. He got it when he jumped off the top of a *supermarket*. He thought he could fly.

He said he really believed he would fly. "For a second or two I thought I was flying. But then the wings *broke,*" he said. He was lucky to get away with only a broken nose.

He is going to try to fly again. "Next time I'll need a 20-foot wing. A 10-foot wing was too short."

Walter is a big, strong man. Once a 252-*pound* man jumped on his *chest* from six feet away. Walter was not hurt.

He tells how he first found out how strong he was. "I was walking along the street when I saw a *child trapped* under a car. So I *lifted* the car up."

Another time 15 men sat on his back. He lifted them up, too. He was asked if he had any *advice* for other people. He said, "If you don't know how to put your head through a *brick wall,* don't try."

—MILWAUKEE JOURNAL

CHECK YOUR UNDERSTANDING

1. When Walter Cornelius jumped from the top of a supermarket
   (a) he flew a hundred yards through the air.
   (b) he was not hurt at all.
   (c) he broke his nose.

2. Next time Walter tries to fly
   (a) he'll use 10-foot wings.
   (b) he'll use 20-foot wings.
   (c) he won't use wings.

3. Walter *first* found out how strong he was when
   (a) he lifted a car with a child trapped under it.
   (b) a 252-pound man jumped on his chest.
   (c) he lifted 15 men sitting on his back.

4. Walter's advice in the last paragraph means:
   (a) Stay away from brick walls.
   (b) Don't try to do something you can't do.
   (c) Don't try to do anything with your head.
5. Another title that would best explain the main idea of this story is:
   (a) Getting a Broken Nose
   (b) A Strong Man Who Didn't Fly
   (c) Saving a Trapped Child

FIND THE MISSING WORD

In your notebook, complete the following sentences with words from the story. You may look back at the story.

1. He jumped off the top of a . . . .
2. A 252-pound man jumped on his . . . .
3. Walter saw a child . . . . under a car.
4. If you don't know how to put your head through a . . . . wall don't try.
5. He was asked if he had any . . . . for other people.

FIRST THINGS FIRST

Arrange these events in the order in which they really happened.

1. Walter broke his nose.
2. Walter jumped off the top of a supermarket.
3. The wings broke.
4. For a second or two, Walter thought he was flying.

IMPROVING YOUR VOCABULARY

Fill in the blank space in each sentence with the word from Column B that best fits. Use each word in Column B only once.

A	B
1. Mrs. Jones complained that her children did not listen to her	(a) broke
2. We watched in surprise as Walter . . . . the car off the ground.	(b) trapped
3. The man was . . . . and could not get himself free.	(c) advice
4. Gus . . . . his leg and had to be taken to the hospital.	(d) child
5. A little . . . . came running in front of the bus.	(e) lifted

WORD BUILDING

Syllables

A. Divide these words into syllables. If the word has only one syllable, copy it and put a circle around it.

1. problem
2. market
3. advice
4. pennies
5. chest

When there is one consonant between two vowels, the word is usually divided before the consonant. For example, *today* is divided as *to day*. In *today,* the consonant *d* is between two vowels *o* and *a*. You divide the word *to-day* before the *d: to day*.

B. Divide each of these words into syllables:

1. July
2. before
3. places
4. broken
5. stolen

EXPRESSING YOURSELF

1. How could a man as strong as Walter Cornelius earn his living? List ten jobs at which he could succeed.

2. Some might think that a man who jumps off a building with wings on his back is mentally sick. Suppose there is nothing wrong with him, however. Why then would he do something as dangerous as that?

3. If you heard someone using the name "Samson" in telling about Walter Cornelius, what would he mean?

4. If you could fly like a bird, where would you go? What kind of life would you lead? Write a few sentences giving your answer to these questions.

14. HIS LAST TRIP

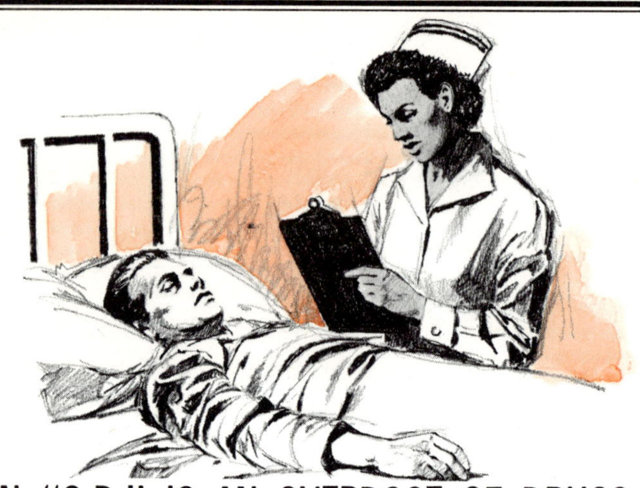

AN "O.D." IS AN OVERDOSE OF DRUGS. PEOPLE DIE FROM AN "O.D." AND THE END IS NOT PRETTY

WHAT DOES DON CHASE'S DEATH TELL YOU ABOUT DRUGS?

MILWAUKEE, Wisc.,–An *inquest* * Thursday into the *death* of a young man told the story of what is it like to die from *drugs*.

The inquest *records* showed that Don Chase "freaked out" during questioning on December 7th in the police station. When police asked him whether he wanted to see a doctor, Don answered, "Man, I'm really *enjoying* it."

* inquest–an attempt to find out the facts regarding a sudden death.

Don was taken to County General Hospital at 6:45 A.M. At 8:45 A.M. his *temperature* was 107.

Hospital records show his *condition* this way:

"Patient's skin is very *pale* and wet; skin under nails blue; eyes rolling; patient had *shakes;* went into a fit; patient tied down.

"9:25 A.M. – *heart* beat not even . . .

9:35 A.M. – heart beat 160 beats per minute (two times that of a good beat)

9:40 A.M. – heart beat slowing down

9:45 A.M. – dead."

The inquest records showed that too much of a drug called MDA caused the death of Don Chase, 18. He was the son of Mr. and Mrs. S. Chase of Parish, Louisiana.

—MILWAUKEE JOURNAL

CHECK YOUR UNDERSTANDING

1. Don's temperature reached a high of
   (a) 110 degrees.
   (b) 107 degrees.
   (c) 103 degrees.

2. The police tried to
   (a) find out what was wrong with Don.
   (b) put Don in jail.
   (c) help Don's parents.

3. Don died from
   (a) a skin rash.
   (b) too much of a drug called MDA.
   (c) a bad heart.

4. "Freaked out" means
   (a) the police found Don.
   (b) Don tried to get out of jail.
   (c) Don was high on drugs.

5. Another title that would best explain the main idea of this story is:
   (a) The Drug Market
   (b) Happiness is Popping Pills
   (c) A Painful Death

FIND THE MISSING WORD

In your notebook, complete the following sentences with words from the story. You may look back at the story.

1. The city held an . . . . Thursday into the death of a young man.
2. At the hospital he had a very high . . . .
3. The hospital records tell about his . . . .
4. The . . . . skin was pale and wet.
5. His . . . . beat was 160 beats per minute.

FIRST THINGS FIRST

Arrange these events in the order in which they really happened to Don Chase.

1. His skin became very wet and pale.
2. He was taken to a hospital.
3. His heart beat was not even.
4. He was dead at 9:45.
5. An inquest was held into his death.

IMPROVING YOUR VOCABULARY

Fill in the blank space in each sentence with the word from Column B that best fits. Use each word in Column B only once.

A	B
1. When you are afraid, your .... beats fast.	(a) patient
2. His school .... show that Freddy was a good student.	(b) heart
3. Rodney was so cold he started to .... all over.	(c) enjoying
4. Time goes fast when you are .... yourself.	(d) shake
5. The doctor said that Leroy was the worst .... he had ever had.	(e) records

WORD BUILDING

Syllables

Divide these words into syllables.

1. began
2. taken
3. places
4. wedding
5. party

Vowel Sounds

When you see a word that ends in *e*, that *e* is usually silent. It gives a signal that the vowel before the consonant is long in most one-syllable words. For example, in the word *ape,* the *e* is silent, and the *a* is long. In the word *fire,* the *e* is silent, and the *i* is long.

A. Fill in the blanks in each sentence.

1. In the word *made,* the .... is silent and the .... is long.
2. In the word *stole,* the .... is long and the .... is silent.
3. In the word *use,* the .... is silent and the .... is long.
4. In the word *hope,* the .... is long and the .... is silent.
5. In the word *take,* the .... is silent and the .... is long.

B. Below are five pairs of words. Choose the word from each pair that has a long vowel sound and copy it in your notebook.

1. like	list
2. wet	eve
3. chase	pass
4. dope	not
5. cute	cut

EXPRESSING YOURSELF

1. Make a list of all the things which your school is doing to fight the drug problem. Tell which is the most important of them all.
2. A doctor said, "If any kid is thinking about messing with drugs, he should visit our hospital and see how sick a suffering addict can be." If

all young people could see such painful sights, do you think that would keep them from ever using drugs?

3. The story does not tell us *why* Don Chase turned to drugs. Make believe you know the reasons and tell about them in a paragraph.
4. Should marijuana be legalized? Explain.
5. Tell about someone who had a bad trip with drugs.

15. HE'D RATHER SWEEP FLOORS

LOSE $650 A MONTH TO STAND BY SOMETHING YOU BELIEVE IN?

WAS LEROY BATES RIGHT IN DOING WHAT HE DID?

FT. LAUDERDALE, Fla. (AP) – Leroy Bates is a college *graduate*. Yet, he *sweeps* floors for about $40 a week. He says he would rather push a *broom* than say the *Pledge* of *Allegiance* to the Flag.

Bates is 25 years old. He was a teacher in Florida. A few weeks ago he was fired for not joining his students in the Pledge to the Flag.

Bates said he could not say the Pledge because of the words *"liberty* and *justice* for all." He said these words are not true for black people in the U.S.A. Leroy Bates is black.

He said he would like very much to return to teaching. "But I feel a man should be able to do what he wants as long as it's within the *law."*

Bates had made about $800 a month, more than four times what he is making now. He says his wife was *upset* when he was fired, but that she *understands* now. They have two young children.

—LOS ANGELES TIMES

CHECK YOUR UNDERSTANDING

1. Leroy Bates now makes
  (a) $800 a month.
  (b) $3,200 a month.
  (c) less than $200 a month.

2. Leroy Bates sweeps floors because
  (a) he is a college graduate.
  (b) he likes that kind of work.
  (c) he was fired from his job.

3. Leroy Bates lost his job because
  (a) he was a black man.
  (b) he would not say the Pledge of Allegiance.
  (c) he doesn't like teaching.

4. Leroy Bates could not say the Pledge of Allegiance because
  (a) he felt the words were not true for black people.
  (b) he did not know the words.
  (c) he feels it's against the law.

5. Another title that best explains the main idea of this story is:

(a) A College Graduate Teaches School
(b) Black Man Gives up Job for What He Believes In
(c) The Pledge of Allegiance in Schools

FIND THE MISSING WORD

In your notebook, complete the following sentences with words from the story. You may look back at the story.

1. Leroy Bates is a college . . . .
2. He . . . . floors for about $40 a week.
3. He was fired for not joining his students in the . . . . to the flag.
4. He could not say the Pledge because of the words, ... and justice for all.
5. His wife was . . . . when he was fired.

FIRST THINGS FIRST

Arrange these events in the order in which they really happened to Leroy Bates.

1. He was fired from his job.
2. He got a job sweeping floors.
3. He did not salute the flag in school.
4. He graduated from college.
5. He got a job as a teacher.

IMPROVING YOUR VOCABULARY

Fill in the blank space in each sentence with the word from Column B that best fits. Use each word in Column B only once.

A	B
1. His wife was .... when he lost his job.	(a) understands
2. David .... why you couldn't come to his party, and he is not angry with you.	(b) liberty
3. He sweeps the floor with the ....\.	(c) graduate
4. The Pledge of Allegiance calls for .... and justice for all.	(d) broom
5. Kenny is a college ...., but he cannot find a job.	(e) upset

---

WORD BUILDING

Syllables

Divide these words into syllables. If the word has only one syllable, copy it and put a circle around it.

1. doctor
2. like
3. enjoy
4. upset
5. better

Vowel Sounds

Sometimes two vowels stand next to one another in a word. When this happens, the first vowel is usually long and the second vowel is silent. These vowels are not separated when the word is broken up into syllables. For example, here are double vowels that you will see in many words:

a i in words like *r a i n*

o a in words like *c o a t*
e e in words like *k e e p*

Say each word. Then cross out the silent vowel.

1. pain
2. sweep
3. teach
4. boat
5. soak

More to do. Divide these words into syllables:

1. repeat
2. disease
3. receive
4. complain
5. again

EXPRESSING YOURSELF

1. If the Pledge of Allegiance were changed to read, "One nation, *seeking* liberty and justice for all," do you think Leroy Bates would agree to saying that?

2. Make believe that you are a reporter getting a story from Mr. Bates. Write out three good questions which you would ask him. Act out this interview with a friend.

3. Imagine you are the wife of Leroy Bates. Would you understand his action? If he were your father, would you be proud of him?

4. About six weeks after this story was written, the MIAMI HERALD told of a judge ordering the school board to return Mr. Bates to his teaching job. The judge said that Bates "may be in fact more patriotic than some other people who push their patriotism in other ways." What did the judge mean by that?

5. Do you agree with the school board that Leroy Bates should have been fired? Or do you agree with the judge who ordered that he be returned to his job?

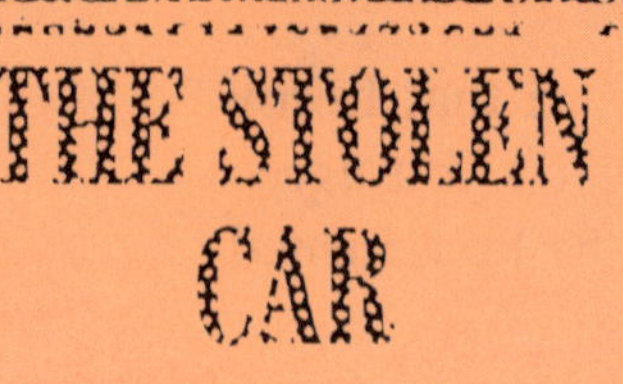

REVIEW OF LESSONS 11-15

FINDING THE MISSING WORD

The sentences below are followed by a list of *italicized* words. For each sentence, write the word that fits best in the blank. Use each word only once. (The number in parentheses tells you the number of the story in which the word was first used.)

1. We went shopping in the ....
2. Bob will need an .... on his broken leg.
3. That old watch is not .... very much.
4. Carla's .... beat fast as she saw her father again after twenty years.
5. The boy died from an overdose of ....

6. Maria carried a .... onto the airplane.
7. The school .... were lost in the fire.
8. You have to .... the can before drinking the tomato juice.
9. Hector made only one .... on his math test.
10. Rita ate so much she gained a ....

(a) *mistake* (12) (f) *records* (14)
(b) *suitcase* (12) (g) *drugs* (14)
(c) *heart* (14) (h) *worth* (11)
(d) *shake* (14) (i) *supermarket* (13)
(e) *pound* (13) (j) *operation* (11)

FINDING THE OPPOSITE

For each of the *italicized* words, choose the word on the right that is most nearly opposite. (The number in parentheses tells you the number of the story in which the word was first used.)

1. *broke* (13) (a) raised; (b) repaired; (c) smashed
2. *child* (13) (a) adult; (b) woman; (c) man
3. *death* (14) (a) height; (b) freedom; (c) life
4. *enjoying* (14) (a) helping; (b) disliking; (c) repairing
5. *justice* (15) (a) unfairness; (b) freedom; (c) truth
6. *loaded* (12) (a) lifted; (b) shook; (c) dumped
7. *lying* (11) (a) breaking; (b) standing; (c) speaking
8. *patient* (14) (a) policeman; (b) doctor; (c) lawyer

9. *trapped* (13) — (a) freed; (b) lost; (c) told
10. *upset* (15) — (a) new; (b) mistaken; (c) calm

UNSCRAMBLING THE WORD

Each of the definitions below is followed by a scrambled word that fits the meaning. Unscramble the letters to find the word. (The number in parentheses tells you the number of the story in which the word was first used.)

1.	opinion about what should be done (13)	VDAEIC
2.	field for airplanes to land on (12)	PATROIR
3.	taken to jail or court (11)	RRSEDETA
4.	hitting again and again (11)	AGTIBNE
5.	brush with a long handle (15)	ROOMB
6.	the school after high school (11)	EELLOCG
7.	without much color (14)	LEAP
8.	money given to help a student go on with studies (12)	HPHISLOCRAS
9.	to clean with a broom (15)	EPSWE
10.	degree of heat or cold (14)	ARTUTEEPMRE

FINDING THE RIGHT MEANING

For each of the *italicized* words, choose its correct meaning from the choices on the right. (The number in parentheses tells you the number of the story in which the word was first used.)

1. *cab* (12) (a) young lion; (b) taxi; (c) auto
2. *condition* (14) (a) something which is found in the kitchen; (b) state in which a person or thing is; (c) number of persons or things together
3. *group* (11) (a) firm hold on something; (b) number of persons or things together; (c) side of a house or room
4. *hospital* (11) (a) place for the care of the sick; (b) large balloon; (c) place for men to join the army
5. *liberty* (15) (a) freedom; (b) slavery; (c) operation
6. *lifted* (13) (a) dropped; (b) raised; (c) thrown
7. *often* (12) (a) never; (b) always; (c) many times
8. *study* (12) (a) to try to learn; (b) to keep calm; (c) to send away
9. *understand* (15) (a) to stay next to; (b) to run from; (c) to get the meaning of
10. *wall* (13) (a) floor of a house; (b) top of a house; (c) side of a house

WRAPPING IT UP:
A REVIEW OF LESSONS 1-15

HOW DOES FOLK SINGER LORETTA LYNN FEEL ABOUT THE PEOPLE FROM "BACK HOME"?

"I was born a coal miner's daughter, in a cabin on a hill in Butcher Holler."

That's how life began for Loretta Lynn. She left the coal fields of Eastern Kentucky to become a country music star. But she hasn't forgotten the people back home. She hasn't forgotten how poor they are, or how dangerous it is to work the mines.

So she's busy now, getting together a big country music show. All the money from the show will go to the wives and children of 38 miners killed two months ago in a mine explosion.

Loretta Lynn still talks and sings with a strong mountain accent. She wrote a hit song, "Coal Miner's Daughter." That song is the story of her own early life in Kentucky.

"I grew up in Butcher Holler," she said. "My daddy was

... Maybe he thou... witch," the dark-eyed woman said. Without any hate she told about her experiences.

Until three years before, Kasmanjari was of normal height. She had been married for many years. There were no children, but she and her husband were happy.

Suddenly, Kasmanjari started growing taller. In two or three months, she added four to five inches to her height. "Everyone in the village saw the change. I was stared at and made fun of. When I went to shop, children would follow me chanting, 'Tall woman, tall woman, you are like the mango tree.' I was even stoned once by some old women."

By last year Kasmanjari was almost nine feet tall. There was no end to the poor woman's bad luck. Her husband had left her. Her brothers' wives turned against her. They said that she was evil. They blamed the death of a child in the family on her. One night she took what she owned and began wandering.

Doctors said she had an illness in the part of the body that controls growth. They said there was no cure. "The doctors do not think I will live many more years," she says simply.

"I hope the end comes soon. I am not afraid of death—I look forward to it," she said, drying her red and yellow sari on the banks of the Ganges ...

Orang...

Orange people? People ... color of the orange you e...

A doctor told of a man w... had come to him for help. T... man had been living in Ala... for three years. He thou... he was not getting enough s... light there. He ate about f... carrots a day. He drank ... large can of tomato ju... every three days. He also ... lots of yellow vegetables.

Too many carrots, tomat... and yellow vegetables cau... him to turn orange.

The cure was simple. ... doctor told the man to ...

THE STOLE... CAR

CANTON, Ohio (AP) One morning at the police ... tion, Policeman Ed Red... received a call. The caller ... he had just stolen a car.

"Is that so? How com..." Redding asked.

"Well," said the man, "... taking a walk. I see this ... Its motor is running and ... body is in it. I thought that ... fool that leaves his car on ... street like that deserves

FINDING THE MISSING WORD

Write the *italicized* word from below each sentence that fits best into the blank space.

1. We .... the milk from the coconut.
(a) *ate;* (b) *kicked;* (c) *drank;* (d) *helped*

2. Lionel grew four .... in one month.
(a) *inches;* (b) *records;* (c) *suitcases;* (d) *minds*

3. Mia wore sweet-smelling ....
(a) *airport;* (b) *perfume;* (c) *nobody;* (d) *company*

4. John went to Mexico and became .... in that country.
(a) *caused;* (b) *repeated;* (c) *answered;* (d) *interested*

5. The cut on Mike's hand drew ....
(a) *ad;* (b) *pound;* (c) *blood;* (d) *heart*

6. Ruth made only one .... on her English test.
(a) *mistake;* (b) *manager;* (c) *church;* (d) *airport*

7. The .... is on the left side of the body.
(a) *law;* (b) *thirty;* (c) *mistake;* (d) *heart*

8. The .... is the outer cover of the body.
(a) *heart;* (b) *skin;* (c) *blood;* (d) *gas*

9. Martin did not know what to do about his ....
(a) *thunderstorm;* (b) *problem;* (c) *police;* (d) *smoke*

10. The .... of Doris and Bill will take place in June.
(a) *record;* (b) *cigarette;* (c) *suitcase;* (d) *wedding*

11. When Tina found her suitcase missing, she called the ....
(a) *mistake;* (b) *dead;* (c) *police;* (d) *coconut*

12. A .... was loose in the outside wall.
(a) *problem;* (b) *creek;* (c) *brick;* (d) *beer*

13. Larry and Dave had many things in ....
(a) *million;* (b) *common;* (c) *manager;* (d) *color*

14. There are .... days in the month of June.
(a) *fifty;* (b) *hospital;* (c) *temperature;* (d) *thirty*

15. Tom likes the .... he works for.
(a) *company;* (b) *original;* (c) *refrigerator;* (d) *wedding*

16. On the bottle it said to .... well before using.
(a) *shake;* (b) *dump;* (c) *sweep;* (d) *drink*

17. The stamp was .... fifty dollars.
(a) *wrinkled;* (b) *stolen;* (c) *worth;* (d) *having*

18. The .... of the team told Ira to go in to pitch.
(a) *dream;* (b) *manager;* (c) *oil;* (d) *justice*

19. Harry ate so much he had a pain in his ....
(a) *cause;* (b) *creek;* (c) *pound;* (d) *stomach*

20. After high school, Don hopes to go to ....
(a) *newspaper;* (b) *condition;* (c) *college;* (d) *allegiance*

21. Gordon is unhappy because his bike was ....
(a) *ripest;* (b) *stolen;* (c) *beaten;* (d) *good*

22. Alice .... from school next year.
(a) *graduates;* (b) *smash;* (c) *dream;* (d) *sweep*

23. We went to the .... to watch the planes fly in and out.
(a) *college;* (b) *hospital;* (c) *airport;* (d) *bay*

24. We read a review of the movie in the ....
(a) *month;* (b) *newspaper;* (c) *company;* (d) *funeral*

25. He was only twelve, but his .... was that of a 90-year-old man.
(a) *carrot;* (b) *taxi;* (c) *crops;* (d) *body*

FINDING THE OPPOSITE

For each of the *italicized* words, choose the word on the right that is most nearly opposite. (The number in parentheses tells you the number of the story in which the word was first used.)

1. *arrives* (6)	(a) leaves; (b) finds; (c) buys
2. *bride* (10)	(a) father; (b) groom; (c) patient
3. *broke* (13)	(a) repaired; (b) received; (c) freed
4. *child* (13)	(a) fellow; (b) adult; (c) body
5. *cool* (1)	(a) warm; (b) tight; (c) well
6. *crooked* (9)	(a) loose; (b) trapped; (c) straight
7. *die* (3)	(a) fall; (b) live; (c) break
8. *discovered* (7)	(a) lost; (b) pushed; (c) drank
9. *dry* (3)	(a) sandy; (b) common; (c) wet
10. *enjoying* (14)	(a) finding; (b) lying; (c) disliking
11. *fellow* (10)	(a) brown; (b) girl; (c) ad
12. *forward* (6)	(a) straight; (b) tight; (c) backward
13. *loose* (1)	(a) tight; (b) simple; (c) upset

14. *lying* (11) (a) standing; (b) trying; (c) fooling
15. *nobody* (4) (a) nothing; (b) everybody; (c) nowhere
16. *patient* (14) (a) captain; (b) doctor; (c) manager
17. *received* (4) (a) lifted; (b) left; (c) gave
18. *sick* (6) (a) well; (b) dizzy; (c) pale
19. *simple* (5) (a) hard; (b) cool; (c) thirsty
20. *student* (8) (a) school; (b) teacher; (c) pupil
21. *trapped* (13) (a) caught; (b) broke; (c) freed
22. *truth* (4) (a) law; (b) lie; (c) life
23. *upset* (15) (a) calm; (b) loose; (c) common
24. *war* (10) (a) battle; (b) dream; (c) peace
25. *whole* (6) (a) past; (b) path; (c) part

UNSCRAMBLING THE WORD

Each of the definitions below is followed by a scrambled word that fits the meaning. Unscramble the letters to find the word. (The number in parentheses tells you the number of the story in which the word was first used.)

1. opinion about what should be done (13) CEDAIV
2. too (5) SOAL
3. taken to jail or court (11) RADTERES
4. small closed place for a telephone (4) OOHBT
5. brush with long handle (15) ROMBO
6. taxi (12) ACB

7. small stream (8) RKECE
8. to make a picture of (7) RWDA
9. person without sense (4) OFLO
10. to make one act against his will (6) CFREO
11. anything that can be burned to make heat or power (2) LEFU
12. something put into automobiles to make them run (2) SGA
13. the seventh month (3) YJLU
14. something that is worthless (8) UJKN
15. something to be carried (12) ODAL
16. one of 12 periods of time into which a year is divided (9) TMHON
17. without much color (14) PLEA
18. a kind of tree that grows in warm places (1) APLM
19. to break into pieces (1) AMSSH
20. to act like one who is ashamed to be seen (7) ANKES
21. to smell (2) FFINS
22. to clean with a broom (15) WPESE
23. part of the mouth used for biting and chewing (9) ETETH
24. juicy, round, red fruit used as a vegetable (5) MTOOTA
25. side of a house or room (13) LALW

FINDING THE RIGHT MEANING

For each of the *italicized* words, choose its correct meaning from the choices on the right. (The number in parentheses tells you the number of the story in which the word was first used.)

1. *age* (9) (a) time of life; (b) part of whole; (c) side of house

2. *battle* (8) — (a) peace; (b) fight; (c) wish

3. *captain* (7) — (a) slave; (b) army; (c) leader

4. *cause* (3) — (a) person, thing, or event that makes something happen; (b) part of a machine that makes it go; (c) speech made against someone

5. *complain* (2) — (a) to tell the reason; (b) to ask for help; (c) to say that something is wrong

6. *condition* (14) — (a) part of the body which receives eaten food; (b) state in which a person or thing is; (c) opinion on what should be done

7. *crops* (3) — (a) statements that are not true; (b) trees that grow in warm countries; (c) plants grown by people for their use

8. *cure* (5) — (a) to make well; (b) to speak ill of; (c) to force

9. *deserve* (4) — (a) to want very much; (b) to have a right to; (c) to run away from

10. *disease* (9) — (a) sickness; (b) luck; (c) peace

11. *dump* (8) — (a) to make wet; (b) to throw out; (c) to set free

12. *during* (10) — (a) just before; (b) at the end of; (c) through the whole time of

13. *group* (11) — (a) number of persons or things together; (b) one person or thing; (c) no persons or things

14. *hospital* (11)	(a) field where airplanes take off and land; (b) place for the care of the sick; (c) place where people come to study
15. *liberty* (15)	(a) happiness; (b) illness; (c) freedom
16. *lifted* (13)	(a) raised; (b) remained; (c) lowered
17. *motor* (4)	(a) top of a car; (b) place where cars can stop; (c) part of a car that makes it go
18. *often* (12)	(a) few times; (b) many times; (c) not at all
19. *pains* (6)	(a) feelings of hurt; (b) sharp, pointed things; (c) pots used for cooking
20. *soldier* (10)	(a) captain in the air force; (b) man who serves in the army; (c) kind of ship used in war
21. *study* (12)	(a) to stay even; (b) to try hard; (c) to try to learn
22. *thirsty* (1)	(a) wanting to drink; (b) 30 years old; (c) able to be trusted
23. *understand* (15)	(a) to get the meaning of; (b) to try again; (c) to stay under
24. *wore* (3)	(a) had for dinner; (b) had on the body; (c) had trouble with
25. *worried* (3)	(a) wore; (b) worn; (c) uneasy

16. UNDERCOVER POLICEMAN LOSES FRIENDS

A DETECTIVE SAID, "A FRIEND WHO SELLS DRUGS IS NO LONGER A FRIEND." WHAT DID HE MEAN?

SHOULD YOU TURN IN YOUR FRIENDS BECAUSE THEY USE OR PUSH DRUGS?

NORFOLK, Va., Jan 2 (AP) – Rick Snively's first *job* as a policeman was to join some drug-using groups.

He let his hair grow long. He got a job as a *trumpet* player with a *hippie* band. At times he was in *danger* when drug pushers wanted him to take drugs in front of them.

Because of his work, 54 drug users and pushers were arrested. But, also because of his work, Rick lost most of his friends.

When he leaves for work each morning, he drives over painted black letters *spelling* PIG in the street in front of his house. At night he *circles* the block to make sure no one is waiting to get him. As soon as he *enters* anyplace where his old high school friends hang out, it *becomes* quiet.

Still, Rick says he would do it all over again. There is still a drug problem, even with the 54 arrests he brought about.

He received a call from the mother of one of the young people arrested as drug users. The mother *praised* Rick and his work. She told him it was a "wonderful thing" because her *son* was now getting help.

—LOS ANGELES TIMES

CHECK YOUR UNDERSTANDING

1. On Rick Snively's first job as a policeman, he had to
   (a) become a drug pusher.
   (b) get a job as a trumpet player.
   (c) tell everyone he was a policeman.

2. Because of his work, Rick Snively
   (a) lost most of his friends.
   (b) lost his job.
   (c) got a job with a better band.

3. Rick Snively says
   (a) the drug problem is gone because of his work.
   (b) he would do it all over again.
   (c) everybody likes him because of the work he did.
4. The mother of one of the young people arrested
   (a) did not like Rick.
   (b) said her son was not getting help.
   (c) praised Rick and his work.
5. Another title that would best explain the main idea of this story is:
   (a) His First Job
   (b) Playing Trumpet for a Hippie Band
   (c) He Made the Arrests, But Lost His Friends

FIND THE MISSING WORD

In your notebook, complete the following sentences with words from the story. You may look back at the story.

1. At times he was in .... when drug pushers wanted him to take drugs in front of them.
2. Because of his work, 54 people were ....
3. He drives over painted black letters .... PIG.
4. At night he .... the block to make sure no one is waiting to get him.
5. Things become quiet as soon as he .... anyplace.

FIRST THINGS FIRST

Arrange these events in the order in which they really happened to Rick Snively.

1. He lost most of his friends.
2. He became a policeman.
3. A mother of one of the young people he arrested praised him and his work.
4. Because of his work, 54 drug users and pushers were arrested.
5. He got a job as a trumpet player with a hippie band.

IMPROVING YOUR VOCABULARY

Fill in the blank space in each sentence with the word from Column B that best fits. Use each word in Column B only once.

A	B
1. When he .... the room, everyone is quiet.	(a) danger
2. Fran lost her .... because she kept coming late.	(b) enters
3. When you drive too fast, you are in .... of losing your life.	(c) son
4. Mr. Wilson's .... is captain of our school football team.	(d) praised
5. Everyone .... Miriam for her quick thinking.	(e) job

WORD BUILDING

Vowel Sounds

A. Say each word. Then cross out the silent vowel.

1. paint
2. street
3. road
4. praise
5. three

Sometimes two vowels that are next to each other will blend or mix into one sound. These vowels are not separated when a word is broken up into syllables. For example, here are vowels that blend into one sound: *a u* in words like *t a u g h t, o i* in words like *o i l,* and *o o* in words like *f o o l.*

B. Say each word. Then circle the double vowels that blend into one sound.

1. cause
2. pause
3. join
4. tool
5. boil

Syllables

Divide these words into syllables. If the word has only one syllable, copy it and put a circle around it.

1. enters
2. raincoats
3. pain
4. become
5. waitress

EXPRESSING YOURSELF

1. What is your opinion of Rick Snively?
2. Why did the mother of one of the arrested drug users praise Rick for his work? How would most parents act if their children were arrested for drug use?
3. Imagine Rick Snively trying to start up a conversation with one of his old high school friends. Write down what you think the conversation might be like. Use the dialogue form.

17. BLUE SKY OVER TOKYO

WHY DO SOME SAY THAT MAN IS HIS OWN WORST ENEMY?

REMEMBER THE CREEK IN ATLANTA?
WHY IS IT LIKE THE AIR
OVER TOKYO?

About 500 years ago a great man lived in Japan. His name was Ota Dokan. He *built* a home on a *bay*. A busy little town grew up around that bay. Ota *wrote* a *poem* telling about his beautiful home:

This house of *mine*
Is next to many *pine* trees
Sitting on the blue sea,
And from its roof can be seen
The great mountain of Fuji.

The little town that began 500 years ago is today the great city of Tokyo. Over 11 million people live there. No other city in the world has so many people.

Today Ota's poem is remembered with sadness. The pine trees he wrote about died of *pollution.* The blue sea is *poisoned* by the smoke from the city. The beautiful mountain of Fuji can be seen only one day out of ten. Most of the time it cannot be seen because of the deadly *clouds* of carbon monoxide *.

Things are so bad that a swimmer died in the Sumida River. He did not die from drowning. He died from *breathing* in the poisons in the air. One July day 8,000 people went to the hospital because they were ill from the deadly smoke that stayed over the city.

Every big city in the world faces the same problems as Tokyo. Man must do something about these pollution problems now or he will kill himself off. He will not be able to breathe the air or drink the water. He will no longer be able to see the blue sky.

—TIME MAGAZINE

* Carbon monoxide – a deadly gas without color.

CHECK YOUR UNDERSTANDING

1. Ota Dokan
  (a) lives in Japan now.
  (b) is an American.
  (c) lived in Japan 500 years ago.

2. The town that grew up around Ota's house
  (a) is no longer there.
  (b) is now the city of Tokyo.
  (c) sank into the bay.

3. Ota wrote a poem about
   (a) pollution
   (b) his beautiful home.
   (c) Japan.
4. Tokyo today
   (a) has much pollution.
   (b) is just like it was 500 years ago.
   (c) is a small town.
5. Another title that would best explain the main idea of this story is:
   (a) The Dangers of Pollution
   (b) Japan
   (c) The Death of a Swimmer

FIND THE MISSING WORD

In your notebook, complete the following sentences with words from the story. You may look back at the story.

1. He .... a home on a bay.
2. Ota wrote a .... telling about his beautiful home.
3. The pines he wrote about are dead of ....
4. Mt. Fuji cannot be seen because of deadly .... of carbon monoxide.
5. He died from .... in poisons in the air.

WHAT'S THE REASON?

When you read, you sometimes have to be a good detective. You have to find out *why* things happen. See if you can find the right "why" in each of these answers.

1. Ota Dokan's poem is remembered with sadness today because
   (a) Ota is no longer there.
   (b) pollution has killed the beauty of the bay.
   (c) Japanese poets no longer write good poems.
2. The sea is full of poisons because of
   (a) the smoke from the city.
   (b) the fish in it.
   (c) the pine trees.
3. Mt. Fuji cannot be seen because
   (a) it is no longer there.
   (b) tall buildings hide it from sight.
   (c) it is hidden by clouds of carbon monoxide.
4. The swimmer died in the Sumida River because
   (a) he breathed in the poisons of the air.
   (b) he drowned.
   (c) he was killed by a very large fish.

IMPROVING YOUR VOCABULARY

Fill in the blank space in each sentence with the word from Column B that best fits. Use each word in Column B only once.

A	B
1. Jerry .... a long letter to his friend.	(a) breathing
	(b) built
2. Glenn was .... hard at the end of the mile run.	(c) wrote
	(d) clouds
3. They .... a house in the country.	(e) mine
4. This pen is yours and that pen is	

5. The .... in the sky were dark and it looked like rain.

WORD BUILDING

Syllables

A. Divide these words into syllables.

1. because
2. complain
3. toilet
4. joining
5. Milwaukee

When you add *ed* to a word, it counts as a syllable *only* if the word ends in *t* or *d:*

1 Syllable	*2 Syllables*
load	loaded
lift	lifted
1 Syllable	*Still 1 Syllable*
watch	watched

B. Add *ed* to each of these words. Write the number of syllables the new word has.

1. ask
2. jump
3. kill
4. last
5. fold
6. happen
7. arrest
8. discover
9. remember
10. return

EXPRESSING YOURSELF

1. In what way is this story like an earlier one, *Youths Clean Creek?* In that story you learned the word "ecology." How could that word have been used in *Blue Sky Over Tokyo?*
2. If life in big cities such as Tokyo is so unhealthy, why do so many people stay there? Why don't more people move out to the country where the air is clean and fresh?
3. Write a few sentences telling about the condition of the city you live in, or the city nearest you.

18. QUESTION MAN: DID YOU HAVE A HAPPY CHILDHOOD?

O'HARA, THE QUESTION MAN, GOES AROUND EACH DAY ASKING QUESTIONS OF PEOPLE IN SAN FRANCISCO. ONE DAY HE ASKED, "DID YOU HAVE A HAPPY CHILDHOOD?"

WOULD YOU CALL YOUR CHILDHOOD HAPPY?

Mary Sanders, 155 Sansome Street:

Oh, yes! I had a wonderful *childhood*. I grew up in New Orleans. I used to go to the Mardi Gras * in my clown *pajamas*. I'm still having a happy childhood. I've never grown up.

* Mardi Gras – Feast time a few days before Lent.

Dan Randolph, 3258 Market Street:

No, I was brought up in a *state* boarding school in Sparta, Wisconsin. My folks *deserted* me when I was a baby. I tried looking for them but never could find them. I know they were Chippewas.**

Frank Quick, 650 Market Street:

Not *exactly*. I grew up in Mexico City. But things have gotten better all the time. The happiest thing that ever happened to me was when I got *married* five months ago.

Betty Barton, 180 New Montgomery Street:

I grew up in a small town, I was really a *loner* as a child. I was a quiet child. But my parents were really good to me. They were very open and *honest* with me. I've come to *realize* how happy my childhood really was as I've grown older.

Now, what's your opinion? Was your childhood a happy one?

—SAN FRANCISCO CHRONICLE

** Chippewas – an Indian tribe.

CHECK YOUR UNDERSTANDING

1. The Question Man is
   (a) Randolph.
   (b) O'Hara.
   (c) Quick.

2. Betty Barton found out how happy her childhood really was when
   (a) she lived in a small town.
   (b) she got married.
   (c) she grew older.

3. Dan Randolph did not have a happy childhood because
   (a) his folks deserted him.
   (b) he grew up in Mexico City.
   (c) he was a quiet child.
4. Mary Sanders remembers that
   (a) she was brought up in a state boarding school.
   (b) she used to go to the Mardi Gras in clown pajamas.
   (c) she grew up alone.
5. Frank Quick was happiest
   (a) as a child.
   (b) in Mexico City.
   (c) when he got married.

FIND THE MISSING WORD

In your notebook, complete the following sentences with words from the story. You may look back at the story.

1. I had a wonderful ....

2. My parents were open and .... with me.

3. The happiest thing that happened to me was when I got .... five months ago.

4. I've come to .... how happy my childhood really was.

5. My folks .... me when I was a baby.

WHO SAID IT?

Match Column B to Column A.

A	B
1. Betty Barton	A. I used to go to the Mardi Gras.
2. Mary Sanders	B. I know they were Chippewas.
3. Dan Randolph	C. I got married five months ago.
4. Frank Quick	D. I was really a loner as a child.

IMPROVING YOUR VOCABULARY

Fill in the blank space in each sentence in Column A with the word from Column B that fits best. Use each word in Column B only once.

A	B
1. Brenda and Jim got .... when they were both 18.	(a) exactly
2. It was .... 15 feet from the house to the street.	(b) state
3. When all his friends left, Red felt	(c) honest
4. We live in the .... south of New Jersey.	(d) married
5. His students liked Mr. Evans because he was .... and kind.	(e) deserted

WORD BUILDING

Syllables

A. Divide these words into syllables. If the word has only one syllable, put a circle around it.

1. remembered
2. watched
3. wanted
4. tested
5. crooked

When a word ends in a consonant followed by *le,* you divide it into syllables before the consonant: *title* is divided *ti tle.* The consonant before *le* at the end of *title* is *t.* So you divide the word before the consonant *t.*

B. Divide these words into syllables:

1. circle
2. battle
3. table
4. people
5. able
6. simple
7. trouble
8. wrinkle
9. little
10. bottle

EXPRESSING YOURSELF

1. Pretend that you are O'Hara, The Question Man. Ask your friends in school a question and then copy down the answers they give you.

2. What is the happiest memory of your childhood? What is your unhappiest memory? Which memory is clearer in your mind?

3. Which of the four people in this story would you like to know more about? Why?

19. TWO SAVED BY TEENAGER

A "HUNCH" IS A FEELING SOMETHING WILL HAPPEN—EVEN THOUGH IT DOESN'T SEEM LIKELY

HOW DID JIMMY BRAND'S "HUNCH" SAVE HIS BOSS'S LIFE?

AMITYVILLE, N.Y. – Two men are in a hospital here. They are lying in rooms next to one another. Each man *owes* his life to the quick thinking of the same 16-year-old boy.

The boy is Jimmy Brand, a high school student. One of the men he *saved* was his father. The other man was his *boss*. The men were saved at two different times in the same week.

A week ago Jimmy and his father were out driving. His father complained of chest pains. They drove to their doctor. He said Jimmy's father should hurry to the hospital.

But Mr. Brand didn't want to go. Jimmy had to force him to come to the hospital. There, his father had a bad heart *attack*. If he had not been under hospital care he would have died.

Six nights later, on April 16, Jimmy had the night off from his part-time job at Richard Orzano's *grocery* store. He came home about 11 o'clock. But then he *decided* to go out again to check on his boss. For some *reason,* he had a feeling Orzano might be in trouble.

As Jimmy drove up, he saw a man running away from the store. Orzano *staggered* out to Jimmy's car and fell down *against* it. He had been *stabbed*.

"I got him into the car and drove to the hospital," Jimmy said. "It's a 10-minute ride but I got him there in about four minutes."

Jimmy's father and his boss lie in rooms next to one another. They both will live because of Jimmy's quick thinking.

—NEWSDAY (LONG ISLAND, N.Y.)

CHECK YOUR UNDERSTANDING

1. Jimmy's father and Jimmy's boss
   (a) were saved by Jimmy on the same day.
   (b) are in hospital rooms next to one another.
   (c) helped save Jimmy's life.

2. Jimmy's father
   (a) didn't want to go to the hospital.
   (b) was stabbed.
   (c) owns a grocery store.
3. Jimmy's father had a heart attack
   (a) in the car.
   (b) in the hospital.
   (c) in the grocery store.
4. Jimmy's boss
   (a) drove Jimmy to the hospital.
   (b) had a heart attack.
   (c) was stabbed.
5. Another title that would best explain the main idea of this story is:
   (a) Father Saved by Son
   (b) Boss Saved by Worker
   (c) Boy Saves Two Men

FIND THE MISSING WORD

In your notebook, complete the following sentences with words from the story. You may look back at the story.

1. Each man . . . . his life to the quick thinking of the same boy.
2. His father . . . . of chest pains.
3. Jimmy had a part-time job at a . . . . store.
4. He . . . . to go out again to see the store's owner.
5. Orzano . . . . out to Jimmy's car.

FIRST THINGS FIRST

Arrange these events in the order in which they really happened.

1. Jimmy's father had a bad heart attack.
2. Jimmy drove his boss to the hospital.
3. Jimmy's boss was stabbed.
4. Jimmy's father and Jimmy's boss lie in hospital rooms next to one another.
5. The doctor said Jimmy's father should go to the hospital.

IMPROVING YOUR VOCABULARY

Fill in the blank space in each sentence in Column A with the word from Column B that fits best. Use each word in Column B only once.

A	B
1. Jack .... that he would go on to college after high school.	(a) reason
2. Emily had no .... for going there, but she went anyway.	(b) saved
3. In the .... store, Aunt Mary bought milk and eggs.	(c) boss
4. Fernando .... the lives of two people by his quick thinking.	(d) grocery
5. My friend Al works for a .... who is kind and honest.	(e) decided

WORD BUILDING

Syllables

Divide each of these words into syllables.

1. wonderful
2. happy
3. deserted
4. poison
5. waitress

Vowel Sounds

Say each word. Is the italicized vowel long, short, or silent?

1. l*i*fe
2. att*a*ck
3. driv*e*
4. ag*o*
5. pa*i*ns

Consonants

Many words begin with two consonant letters. Here are consonant letters that mix together to make one sound:

sh in words like *show*
ch in words like *child*
wh in words like *what*

For each of the italicized words, choose the word from the three on the right that starts with the same sound.

1.	*what*	(a) well	(b) when	(c) week
2.	*show*	(a) short	(b) sudden	(c) stab
3.	*child*	(a) could	(b) chest	(c) clown
4.	*church*	(a) city	(b) cloud	(c) check
5.	*ship*	(a) skin	(b) state	(c) shinny

EXPRESSING YOURSELF

1. Jimmy had a "feeling" that his boss might be in trouble. Did you ever have a "hunch" that something bad was about to happen? Did it really take place?
2. If you were Jimmy's boss, how would you repay him for saving your life?
3. Write a few sentences about a time when quick thinking saved someone you know who was in danger.

20. WGN PRESENTS . . . A LIVE BANK ROBBERY

RADIO STATIONS ARE ALWAYS LOOKING FOR DIFFERENT KINDS OF PROGRAMS

CAN YOU THINK OF A RADIO PROGRAM AS "DIFFERENT" AS THIS ONE?

SOUTH CHICAGO HEIGHTS, Ill. (AP) – It's a *December* morning. You live in Chicago. You are having breakfast and listening to radio station WGN. There's a real surprise waiting for you. Suddenly you are listening to—a real bank robbery!

WGN radio *reporter* Don Harris received a *tip*. He was told that the police were about to *surround* a bank that was being *robbed*. Harris called the bank. Over the radio, you heard this talk between Harris and the man who answered the telephone:

HARRIS: This is WGN radio. I understand you've got a robbery?
MAN: This is the robber.
HARRIS: Why are you there?
MAN: I want to tell you honestly. I tried to make it the fastest way *possible*, and it's the wrong way.
HARRIS: What's going on now?
MAN: I'm surrounded. I'm going to take my life.
HARRIS: No, don't do that. Wait a second.
MAN: Yeah . . . wait a second.

Shouts from police *rushing* into the bank were heard: "All right, *freeze*. Hands up. Get against the wall."

There was a *clattering* sound. The man had dropped the telephone.

Police later said that the robber had dropped his *gun* and gave himself up. They also said that they had watched the robber through a window as he talked to Harris. They saw him hold a gun to his head at the time he said he was going to kill himself.

WGN received a number of calls from listeners who couldn't believe a bank robber would answer a telephone.

—PHILADELPHIA EVENING BULLETIN

CHECK YOUR UNDERSTANDING

1. Don Harris called the bank because
  (a) he did so every morning.
  (b) the robber was a friend of his.
  (c) he heard that the bank was being robbed.

2. At the time of the phone call, the robber was
  (a) having a gun fight with police.
  (b) glad he had robbed the bank.
  (c) surrounded by police.

3. The clattering sound was caused by
  (a) the robber dropping the phone.
  (b) the police.
  (c) the robber dropping his gun.

4. Most people who called station WGN
  (a) said they liked the show.
  (b) couldn't believe a robber had answered the telephone.
  (c) said Harris never should have called the bank.

5. This story is mainly about
  (a) a radio station and its listeners.
  (b) a talk between a radio reporter and a bank robber.
  (c) people in Chicago who listen to the radio.

FIND THE MISSING WORD

In your notebook, complete the following sentences with words from the story. You may look back at the story.

1. It's a . . . . morning.

2. WGN radio reporter Don Harris received a . . . .

3. He was told that the police were about to .... a bank.
4. Shouts from police .... into the bank were heard.
5. There was a .... sound.

FIRST THINGS FIRST

Arrange these events in the order in which they really happened.

1. The robber gave himself up.
2. Don Harris received a tip that a bank was being robbed.
3. WGN received phone calls from unbelieving listeners.
4. The police rushed into the bank.
5. Harris called the bank.

IMPROVING YOUR VOCABULARY

Fill in the blank space in each sentence in Column A with the word from Column B that fits best. Use each word in Column B only once.

A	B
1. Water will .... when it is below 32°.	(a) possible
	(b) December
2. It isn't .... to do what you ask in such short time.	(c) freeze
	(d) robbed
3. Karen is always .... to make her train.	(e) rushing
4. The last month of the year is	
5. This is the second time that bank has been	

WORD BUILDING

Syllables

Divide each of these words into syllables.

1. raincoat
2. complained
3. hospital
4. student
5. simple

Vowel Sounds

Say each word. Is the italicized vowel long, short, or silent?

1. w*e*ek
2. ch*e*ck
3. *u*sed
4. lon*e*
5. f*u*neral

Consonants

Two consonant letters that are often together at the beginning of a word are *th*. The letter combination *th* may stand for either of two sounds: soft as in *think* or hard as in *this*.

Say each pair of words. If they sound the same at the beginning, write *same*. If they sound different, write *different*. The first one is done for you.

1. then	the	*same*
2. there	they	
3. thunder	think	
4. that	thirty	
5. thing	this	

EXPRESSING YOURSELF

1. How would you act if you were working as a teller in a bank and a robber handed you a note asking for all of your money?
2. Tell about someone you would like to interview. Make up five questions you would like to ask that person.
3. Imagine you are the bank robber. In a few sentences, write:
   (a) why you decided to rob the bank

   or

   (b) your feelings now that you have been caught.

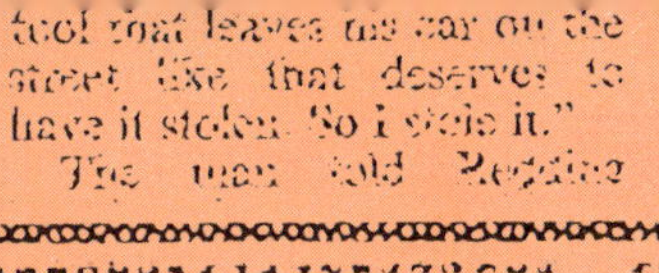

THE STOLEN CAR

CANTON, Ohio (AP) —

ALLAHABAD, India, Chronicle Foreign Service—A
year-old peasant is wandering the streets of Indian towns
cause no one wants to give her shelter. There are thousands
poor begging in this country, but Rasmanjari Rani is unwa
for a strange reason.
Rasmanjari is nearly nine feet tall—one of the tallest wo
in the world.
When she went to a
house the other day, the
locked the door after one
at her.
"Maybe he thought I w
witch," the dark-eyed wo

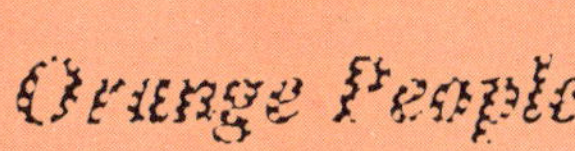

REVIEW OF LESSONS 16-20

FINDING THE MISSING WORD

The sentences below are followed by a list of *italicized* words. For each sentence, write the word that fits best in the blank. Use each word only once. (The number in parentheses tells you the number of the story in which the word was first used.)

1. Angel wants to . . . . a captain in the U.S. Air Force.
2. Peter has a . . . . in the gas station.
3. The words of the song are taken from a beautiful . . . .
4. . . . . of dust were kicked up by the wild horses.
5. The refrigerator is . . . . six feet high.
6. Because of the bad air, Tim had trouble . . . .
7. The man jumped up and . . . . to the wall.
8. Jimmy bought a can of tomato juice in the . . . . store.

9. Dan Harris, a WGN ...., told about a tip he received from a bank robber.
10. I can't believe the crooks .... the candy store.

(a) *breathing* (17)	(f) *exactly* (18)
(b) *become* (16)	(g) *reporter* (20)
(c) *job* (16)	(h) *grocery* (19)
(d) *robbed* (20)	(i) *clouds* (17)
(e) *staggered* (19)	(j) *poem* (17)

FINDING THE OPPOSITE

For each of the *italicized* words, choose the word on the right that is most nearly opposite. (The number in parentheses tells you the number of the story in which the word was first used.)

1. *against* (19)	(a) without; (b) for; (c) by
2. *boss* (19)	(a) owner; (b) worker; (c) tip
3. *clattering* (20)	(a) rattling; (b) loudly; (c) quietly
4. *deserted* (18)	(a) joined; (b) left; (c) surrounded
5. *enters* (16)	(a) finds; (b) leaves; (c) discovers
6. *honest* (18)	(a) open; (b) untruthful; (c) lonely
7. *married* (18)	(a) together; (b) single; (c) tied
8. *possible* (20)	(a) maybe; (b) perhaps; (c) impossible
9. *praised* (16)	(a) blamed; (b) forced; (c) approved
10. *son* (16)	(a) daughter; (b) sister; (c) girl

UNSCRAMBLING THE WORD

Each of the definitions below is followed by a scrambled word that fits the meaning. Unscramble the letters to find the word. (The number in parentheses tells you the number of the story in which the word was first used.)

1.	making words with letters (16)	PINGSELL
2.	to close in on all sides (20)	DROUNRUS
3.	one of the 50 main parts of the United States (18)	TATES
4.	used a pen or pencil to make words (17)	RETOW
5.	the last month of the year (20)	CREMBEED
6.	cause (19)	SRNAOE
7.	type of horn (16)	PERTTUM
8.	belonging to me (17)	IMEN
9.	made free from harm (19)	VASED
10.	begin a fight (19)	CATTAK

FINDING THE RIGHT MEANING

For each of the *italicized* words, choose its correct meaning from the choices on the right. (The number in parentheses tells you the number of the story in which the word was first used.)

1.	*bay* (17)	(a) part of land with sea around it; (b) part of a poem; (c) part of the sea with land around it
2.	*built* (17)	(a) sold; (b) made; (c) crooked

3. *circles* (16) (a) finds fault with; (b) leaves later; (c) goes around

4. *danger* (16) (a) safety; (b) pain; (c) trouble

5. *decide* (19) (a) to turn to; (b) to make up one's mind; (c) to send away

6. *freeze* (20) (a) to turn to ice; (b) to start to drink; (c) to boil quickly

7. *honest* (18) (a) trustful; (b) loveliest; (c) helpless

8. *pollution* (17) (a) condition; (b) perfume; (c) dirt

9. *realize* (18) (a) to forget; (b) to understand; (c) to cause

10. *rushing* (20) (a) taking; (b) worrying; (c) hurrying

21. KISS THE REF

WOULD YOU GET A FOUL IF YOU KISSED THE REFEREE? NO RULE IN KENTUCKY HIGH SCHOOL BASKETBALL SAYS YOU CAN'T

WHY WOULD YOU WANT TO DO IT, ANYWAY? WELL, READ ON.

LEXINGTON, Ky. (AP) – Linda Curtsinger is 18, the same age as most high school *seniors*. She is a beautiful *blond* with a *lovely* smile and a great *figure*.

She's also a basketball *referee*. For real!

"Oh, no," she's quick to say, "it has nothing to do with women's liberation.* I really enjoy being a girl." Linda wanted to become a referee last summer, when she was a helper at a 4-H camp. "We got to kidding about it. The more I thought about it, the more I wanted to do it. I went to a school and had to study a lot, but I passed the test," she said.

Then came the experience.

"I was *yelled* at by a *coach* in my first game," she said, "and one coach wouldn't let me work. He said he wanted somebody with more *experience*." But most of the coaches *accepted* her.

One of these coaches said, "You're a girl until you put on that black and white shirt. Then you're a referee." But with the brief black shorts she wears as part of her dress, the boys in the crowd still know she's a girl. Some of them want her *address* and phone number. Some give long, low whistles.

"The boys in the game really are very nice," Linda said. "They say, 'Yes ma'am,' and run and get the ball for me and things like that."

What if a player tried to kiss her? "I don't know, I guess I'd have to decide what to do if that happened; but I don't think it really ever will," said Linda.

—LOS ANGELES TIMES

* women's liberation—the movement to get equal rights for women.

CHECK YOUR UNDERSTANDING

1. At one game the coach of a team said that
- (a) Linda was a great referee.
- (b) Linda did not have enough experience.
- (c) Linda should not yell.

2. Linda became a referee because
   (a) she thought she would like it.
   (b) her father wanted her to become one.
   (c) she wanted to prove that women could do it.
3. The boys in the crowd
   (a) get the ball for Linda.
   (b) want her to throw basketballs.
   (c) whistle at her.
4. If one of the players tried to kiss Linda, she would
   (a) let them.
   (b) decide what to do then.
   (c) kid them out of it.
5. Another title that would best explain the main idea of this story is:
   (a) The Ref is a Girl
   (b) Coaches Want Girl Refs
   (c) The Kissing Ref

FIND THE MISSING WORD

In your notebook, complete the following sentences with words from the story. You may look back at the story.

1. Would you get a foul if you kissed the ....?
2. Linda is a beautiful .... with a lovely smile.
3. I was .... at by a coach in my first game.
4. One coach wanted somebody with more ....
5. Most coaches .... Linda as a referee.

FIRST THINGS FIRST

Arrange these events in the order in which they really happened to Linda Curtsinger.

1. She became a basketball referee.

2. She decided to become a referee when she was at a 4-H Club.

3. She had to pass a test to become a referee.

4. She was yelled at by a coach.

5. She said she doesn't think she will ever be kissed by a player at a game.

IMPROVING YOUR VOCABULARY

Fill in the blank space in each sentence in Column A with the word from Column B that fits best. Use each word in Column B only once.

A	B
1. The new player needed more .... before he could make the first team.	(a) lovely (b) experience (c) seniors (d) accept (e) referee
2. One of the players yelled at the	
3. All of the boys turned to look at the .... young girl.	
4. Four .... on the school team will not be back next year.	
5. We cannot .... your reason for coming late.	

WORD BUILDING

Consonants

A. Say each word. If the *th* sound at the beginning of a word is like the sound in *th*ink, write *think*. If the *th* sound at the beginning of a word is like the sound in *th*is, write *this*. The first one is done for you.

1. thought *think*
2. then
3. that
4. there
5. they

Words may also begin with two consonants that are blended together so that we hear a little of each sound. They are called beginning blends. Here are blends in which *r* is the second letter:

br (broke)
cr (crops)
dr (drive)
gr (grocery)
tr (trouble)

B. Choose a blend from Column B and add it to one of the incomplete words in the sentences in Column A. Do this for each blend.

A	B
1. Someone really ......*ied* to kiss her.	(a) dr
	(b) cr
2. They ......*ove* the car to the doctor.	(c) tr
	(d) gr
3. The boys in the .....*owd* wanted her address.	(e) br

4. My friend has a job at a . . . . *ocery* store.
5. I was . . . . . . *ought* up in a boarding school.

EXPRESSING YOURSELF

1. What did Linda mean by saying that "it has nothing to do with women's liberation"?
2. Would the fellows on your school's basketball team want to have a woman as a referee? Why might they be unhappy about it? Do you see anything wrong in having a woman as a referee or baseball umpire?
3. Girls, would you want to be a basketball referee or baseball umpire?
4. We see women today holding jobs which were usually done by men—driving taxis, giving haircuts, etc. Tell about a woman you know who works at a job which few women worked at ten or twenty years ago.
5. "Girls should be permitted to play on high school teams." Write a few sentences, giving your opinion on this statement.

22. DO CLOTHES MAKE THE MAN?

DO MOST PEOPLE JUDGE A PERSON BY THE CLOTHES HE WEARS?

SACRAMENTO, Cal. (UPI) – Craig Brown, clean and *neatly* dressed, walked into a *jewelry* store. He asked about a ring he had seen in the window, and he was waited on kindly. He was told that if he needed money he could *borrow* it.

The next day, the same Craig Brown walked into the same store. But this time he was dressed like a hippie and wearing a *beard*. No one would wait on him. When he tried to buy a ring, he was told to leave the store.

Craig, 18, is a student at Consumnes River Junior College. *Usually* he is quiet, neat, and clean. He turned hippie for a week for a psychology * class *lesson.*

He put on an old shirt, a pair of washed-out *pants,* Indian *beads,* a head band and torn shoes. Then he stuck on a wig and a beard. Suddenly, he found himself on the other side of the fence.

Two older persons stopped him as he was shopping "and gave me a real talking to." Two *restaurants* would not sell him food.

But he found some good in being dressed like a hippie. He bought two underground newspapers for 25 cents. Dressed in the usual way, he would have to pay the full 50 cents.

Craig Brown was sad about the way some people felt. "Why does it *matter* whether I wear this or that? I'm still the same person."

—THE DENVER POST

* psychology – the science dealing with the way the mind works.

CHECK YOUR UNDERSTANDING

1. Craig Brown found out that he was waited on faster when

(a) he was neatly dressed.

(b) he was badly dressed.

(c) he showed a card.

2. When Craig Brown wore a beard

(a) most people didn't like him.

(b) he was more friendly.

(c) he was not comfortable.

3. Craig Brown wanted to buy
   (a) pants.
   (b) beads.
   (c) jewelry.
4. Craig Brown believes that
   (a) young people should always dress neatly.
   (b) old people are polite.
   (c) it should not matter what you wear.
5. Another title that would best explain the main idea of this story is:
   (a) Hippies Are People
   (b) The Young and the Old
   (c) Man Judged by Clothes He Wears

FIND THE MISSING WORD

In your notebook, complete the following sentences with words from the story. You may look back at the story.

1. Craig Brown walked into a . . . . store.
2. He was waited on . . . .
3. This time he was wearing a . . . . and dressed like a hippie.
4. He put on a pair of washed-out pants and Indian . . . .
5. Two . . . . would not sell him food.

FIRST THINGS FIRST

Arrange these events in the order in which they really happened to Craig.

1. No one waited on him.
2. He went into a jewelry store dressed neatly.

3. He went into the same jewelry store dressed as a hippie.
4. Two restaurants would not sell him food.
5. He was waited on quickly and kindly.

IMPROVING YOUR VOCABULARY

Fill in the blank space in each sentence in Column A with the word from Column B that fits best. Use each word in Column B only once.

A	B
1. Mr. and Mrs. Rich liked to eat in the best.	(a) lesson
2. I will meet you at the . . . . time, unless you would like to come earlier.	(b) usual
3. I hope you learned a . . . . from your mistake.	(c) borrow
4. Bill tried to . . . . money from all of us.	(d) restaurants
5. Sue's clothes were old, but she was . . . . dressed.	(e) neatly

---

WORD BUILDING

Consonants

A. For each italicized word, choose the word from the three on the right that starts with the same sound.

1. *while*	(a) chose	(b) clouds	(c) which
2. *church*	(a) childhood	(b) slip	(c) shook
3. *short*	(a) surround	(b) chest	(c) shake
4. *thin*	(a) trapped	(b) this	(c) thirty
5. *drugs*	(a) danger	(b) dressed	(c) broom

Here are blends in which *l* is the second letter.

bl (black)
cl (clouds)
fl (flag)
pl (player)
sl (sleep)

B. Choose a blend from Column B and add it to one of the incomplete words in the sentences in Column A. Do this for each blend.

A	B
1. I wore a ....*own* mask.	(a) pl
2. A ....*ond* girl is a referee.	(b) cl
	(c) bl
3. The class says the ...*edge* of Allegiance.	(d) fl
	(e) sl
4. She loves the smell of fresh .....*owers.*	
5. His heart beat was ...*owing* down.	

EXPRESSING YOURSELF

1. Why do people care about the way you look rather than about the kind of person you really are?

2. With the help of some friends, try out Craig Brown's experiment to see if the same things happen to you. Have a well-dressed friend go into a few stores and then have someone in old clothes do the same.

3. What is meant by the saying, "Don't judge a book by its cover"? Use that idea as the first sentence for a paragraph in which you tell how a person was fooled by the way someone or something looked.
4. Should students in school be allowed to dress any way they choose? Would you set up any rules at all? What would they be?

23. COAL MINER'S DAUGHTER

DO MOST PEOPLE WHO BECOME FAMOUS FORGET THOSE THEY GREW UP WITH?

HOW DOES FOLK SINGER LORETTA LYNN FEEL ABOUT THE PEOPLE FROM "BACK HOME"?

"I was *born* a coal *miner's* daughter, in a *cabin* on a hill in Butcher Holler."

That's how life began for Loretta Lynn. She left the coal fields of eastern Kentucky to become a country *music star*. But she hasn't *forgotten* the people back home. She hasn't forgotten how poor they are or how dangerous it is to work the mines.

So she's busy now, getting together a big country music show. All the money from the show will go to the wives and children of 38 miners killed two months ago in a mine *explosion.*

Loretta Lynn still talks and sings with a strong mountain *accent.* She wrote a hit song, "Coal Miner's Daughter." That song is the story of her own early life in Kentucky.

"I grew up in Butcher Holler," she said. "My daddy was a coal miner for 16 years. My husband worked the mines for a while and his daddy was a miner for 45 years.

"A lot of my friends got killed in the mines. I've walked past where they were bringing out the men. There had just been an *accident.* I remember all the *women* and children standing around, mostly crying."

Loretta remembered that "daddy would go out to the mines in the evening. There were eight of us kids, and mommy would read to us just about all night by the oil lamp, until daddy would come home.

"Mommy told me once that each time daddy would leave she'd wonder if he'd ever come back."

She says, "Every penny from the show will go to the children. I'd like to see these kids go through school and college and leave the coal mining country and have a better life. And not have to go in the mines."

—LOUISVILLE COURIER-JOURNAL

CHECK YOUR UNDERSTANDING

1. Loretta Lynn

(a) has forgotten the people back home.

(b) has lost her mountain accent.
(c) is now a country music star.

2. The people Loretta Lynn grew up with
(a) are poor.
(b) are all country music stars now.
(c) no longer work in coal mines.

3. The song "Coal Miner's Daughter"
(a) was written by Loretta Lynn's husband.
(b) is about Loretta Lynn's early life in Kentucky.
(c) was sung by Loretta when she was a little girl.

4. Life in the coal mines is
(a) fun.
(b) easy.
(c) dangerous.

5. The big country music show Loretta Lynn is putting together
(a) is for children of coal miners killed in a mine explosion.
(b) is for Loretta's college education.
(c) is to train young people to work in the mines.

FIND THE MISSING WORD

In your notebook, complete the following sentences with words from the story. You may look back at the story.

1. Loretta Lynn was born in a .... on a hill in Butcher Holler.
2. She hasn't .... the people back home.
3. The miners were killed two months ago in a mine ....

4. She still talks and sings with a strong mountain ....
5. She remembers all the .... and children standing around, mostly crying.

FIRST THINGS FIRST

Arrange these events in the order in which they really happened to Loretta Lynn.

1. Her mother would read to the eight children by an oil lamp.
2. She is putting together a country western show to raise money for children of miners.
3. Her husband worked in the mines.
4. She was born in a cabin on a hill in Butcher Holler.
5. She became a country music star.

IMPROVING YOUR VOCABULARY

Fill in the blank space in each sentence in Column A with the word from Column B that fits best. Use each word in Column B only once.

A	B
1. Rose had .... her books and had to return home for them.	(a) born
	(b) accident
	(c) music
2. Carla liked to listen to country	(d) forgotten
	(e) women
3. The two .... looked alike and could have passed for sisters.	

4. Ed was .... in 1961 and is two years older than his sister.
5. He did not mean to trip you; it was an ....

WORD BUILDING

A. If the blends that begin each pair of words below stand for the same sound, write *same.* If they stand for two different sounds, write *different.*

1.	blond	blue
2.	clatter	clouds
3.	player	priest
4.	dressed	drugs
5.	crying	children

Here are blends in which *s* is the first letter.

sl	(slip)
sm	(smash)
sp	(spelling)
st	(store)
sw	(sweet)

B. Choose a blend from Column B and add it to one of the incomplete words in the sentences in Column A. Do this for each blend.

A	B
1. Don't ....*oke,* Joe.	(a) sw
2. He had to ....*eep* floors.	(b) st
3. I get ....*omach* pains.	(c) sm
4. Drive safely. Go ....*ow.*	(d) sp
5. Please open your ....*elling* books.	(e) sl

EXPRESSING YOURSELF

1. Why is a coal miner's work more dangerous than most other jobs? If a coal miner does not get killed in an accident, what else can happen to shorten his life?
2. Imagine you're a child from a poor neighborhood who grows up and makes good. Would you want to forget the old neighborhood and the people you grew up with? Or would you want to return and help them? Explain.
3. Listen to a Loretta Lynn record. Do you like her style of singing? Why?
4. Tell about your favorite singer.
5. Write the words to a song telling about your childhood.

24. CRISIS CENTER

PEOPLE IN TROUBLE OFTEN HAVE NO PLACE TO GO TO FOR HELP

DOES A "CRISIS CENTER" SEEM LIKE A GOOD IDEA?

LOUISVILLE, Ky. – "I wanted to get out . . . " was the thought running through the mind of a young woman. She wanted to kill herself. She called the Crisis *Center* to tell them. A young *social* worker who works there answered the call.

YOUNG MAN: (remembers the voice of the caller) Will you *hang* on for me?

WOMAN'S VOICE:	(thin and weak) I just don't feel like I can hang on. I've gotten rid of all the *pills* and *stuff*. I thought it would be better by today. I don't feel . . .
YOUNG MAN:	Please, please hang on.
WOMAN'S VOICE:	(weaker) Yeh . . . Yeh . . .
YOUNG MAN:	You must call your doctor. Can you do that now? In the morning?
WOMAN'S VOICE:	Yeh . . . but I don't feel like I'm going to make it.
YOUNG MAN:	You'll be O. K. Look, when you feel like you're at the very end call me. You hear?

By 6:15 that night, he had *completed* the call with the young woman, a *mental* patient. He had *recognized* her voice. She had called before. He was glad that he was able to "talk her down."

The center has around-the-clock *service* for taking care of people's problems. It receives many calls. One night a girl called to say that she would kill her husband when he came home. "Things got hot for a while," the young social worker said. "We stayed on with her for an hour and got her to leave the house. Then the police were sent out to see that nothing happened."

Another night a teenage girl said that she thought someone wanted to shoot her and her boyfriend. She said he had already taken a shot at them. The social worker *advised* the teenager to tell her mother and call the police to arrest the man.

Mrs. Rose Mills, another social worker, said that sometimes people do not want help. "If they are not ready, you're not going to get anywhere with them. Most of the time, though, when people call this number, they're ready."

People who feel they have no place to go for help find it at The Crisis Center.

—LOUISVILLE COURIER-JOURNAL

CHECK YOUR UNDERSTANDING

1. The first young woman called the Crisis Center because
   (a) a young man asked her to call.
   (b) she was going to kill herself.
   (c) she wanted her doctor.

2. The Crisis Center is open each day for
   (a) 8 hours.
   (b) 24 hours.
   (c) 12 hours.

3. When the young social worker finished talking with the young woman, he felt
   (a) sad.
   (b) good.
   (c) angry.

4. Mrs. Rose Mills said that
   (a) most people who call do not need help.
   (b) they cannot help people who are not ready for help.
   (c) all people who call are helped.

5. Another title that would best explain the main idea of this story is:
   (a) Fast Help by Police
   (b) 24-Hour Help
   (c) Social Workers

FIND THE MISSING WORD

In your notebook, complete the following sentences with words from the story. You may look back at the story.

1. A young woman called the Crisis .... to tell them she wanted to kill herself.
2. The center has around-the-clock ....
3. He had .... the voice of the young woman.
4. The young woman was a .... patient.
5. Mrs. Rose Mills works at the center as a .... worker.

WHO SAID IT?

Match Column B to Column A.

A	B
1. The social worker	(a) I've gotten rid of all the pills and stuff.
2. The young mental patient	(b) If they're not ready, you're not going to get anywhere with them.
3. Mrs. Mills	(c) Look, when you feel like you're at the very end call me.

IMPROVING YOUR VOCABULARY

Fill in the blank space in each sentence in Column A with the word from Column B that fits best. Use each word in Column B only once.

A	B
1. He was told to .... his coat in the closet.	(a) completed
2. At first, Teri did not .... an old friend she had not seen for many years.	(b) advised
3. Raquel .... high school in three and a half years.	(c) hang
4. Mr. Sanchez .... Robert to become a doctor.	(d) service
5. I hope I can be of ...... to you.	(e) recognize

WORD BUILDING

Consonants

If the blends that begin each pair of words below stand for the same sound, write *same*. If they stand for two different sounds, write *different*.

1.	sweet	swimmer
2.	player	pledge
3.	grow	crops
4.	show	slow
5.	whistle	while
6.	priest	problem
7.	smiled	smash
8.	thunder	thin
9.	blue	breathing
10.	clouds	clattering

Word Endings

When we want words to say more than one, we usually add *s* to them:

ONE	MORE THAN ONE
kid	kid*s*
vessel	vessel*s*
bride	bride*s*
circle	circle*s*

A. Change the word in italics from one to more than one.

1. The Crisis Center has received many *call.*
2. Loretta Lynn has not forgotten the dangers faced by all the *miner.*
3. Her father was a miner for 16 *year.*
4. There are many coal *field* in Eastern Kentucky.
5. Two *restaurant* would not sell him food.

B. Change these words from more than one to one. The first one is done for you.

1. vegetables *vegetable*
2. brides
3. months
4. managers
5. seniors

EXPRESSING YOURSELF

1. Imagine you are working at a crisis center. Tell about some calls you might receive during a day.

2. Again, you are working at the crisis center. A call comes in from a young man who says that he is planning to throw himself off the roof because of the many troubles he has. What would you say to keep him from harming himself?
3. Write a few sentences about someone you know who needed help. Tell how he or she got (or didn't get) it.

25. UGANDA BASKETBALL COACH

ARE YOU LUCKY TO BE AN AMERICAN?

READ WHAT JAMES ADOA OF UGANDA SAYS

James Adoa looks at all that the *United States* has—and just shakes his head. He sees a *gym* in every school. He sees a *uniform* on every player.

James Adoa comes from the African country of Uganda. Uganda is a country of ten million people. There is only one gym in the whole country. Adoa is the head basketball coach of Uganda.

Living in Uganda isn't easy. Adoa is 26 years old, the oldest of 13 children. He makes $80 a month. He sends $40 of that home to his father and mother. This small, quiet black man might complain, but he does not. He works and hopes and dreams a little.

Adoa is coming to the end of a three-month stay in the United States. He says of the U.S.: "You Americans have the money to do everything. But I don't know if you *appreciate* what you have. The kids, most of all, should appreciate it."

Adoa was *taught* basketball in 1962 by a Peace Corps * coach. He then started the first team at his school. He set up the court himself. He taught the *rules* and the game to his players. Later, a team of his won 31 games in a row.

When Adoa became head coach of Uganda in 1968, there were 60 *outdoor courts* in the whole country. Since then, he has had 140 more built.

He helped bring about the first East African basketball games this year. Uganda, Kenya, Tanzania and Zambia took part. *Soccer* is the big game in Uganda. Adoa would like to make basketball as big a game as soccer, but he says Uganda players don't *practice* hard enough. "O.K., let's go play," they say. Sometimes they don't even come to practice. Great basketball needs more than that.

—LOS ANGELES TIMES

* Peace Corps – A U.S. program to help people in other countries.

CHECK YOUR UNDERSTANDING

1. James Adoa is
   (a) an American basketball player.
   (b) head basketball coach of Uganda.
   (c) a rich man.
2. Adoa thinks that Americans
   (a) have the money to do everything.
   (b) appreciate what they have.
   (c) do not have as much as Uganda.
3. Uganda
   (a) has many gyms.
   (b) is a country in Africa.
   (c) has twenty million people.
4. In Uganda now, there are
   (a) 60 basketball courts.
   (b) 140 basketball courts.
   (c) 200 basketball courts.
5. Another title that would best explain the main idea of this story is:
   (a) Learning Basketball from a Peace Corps Coach
   (b) A Trip to the United States
   (c) He Wants to Make Basketball Big in His Country

FIND THE MISSING WORD

In your notebook, complete the following sentences with words from the story. You may look back at the story.

1. He sees a .... on every player.
2. In 1968, there were 60 .... basketball courts in the whole country.

3. Adoa was .... the game in 1962 by a Peace Corps coach.
4. He taught the .... and the game to his players.
5. He says the Uganda players don't .... hard enough.

FIRST THINGS FIRST

Arrange these events in the order in which they really happened to James Adoa.

1. A team of his won 31 games in a row.
2. He came to America for a three-month stay.
3. He helped bring about the first East African basketball games with Uganda, Kenya, Tanzania, and Zambia.
4. He was taught basketball by a Peace Corps coach.
5. He was made head basketball coach of Uganda.

IMPROVING YOUR VOCABULARY

Fill in the blank space in each sentence in Column A with the word from Column B that fits best. Use each word in Column B only once.

A	B
1. It takes a lot of .... to become a good basketball player.	(a) taught
	(b) courts
	(c) practice
2. We can play on one of the two basketball	(d) gym
	(e) appreciate
3. I .... the help you have given me.	

4. First, the players were .... the rules of the game.
5. In the .... class, we play basketball and run around the indoor track.

WORD BUILDING

Word Endings

A. Change the words on the left from one to more than one. The first one is done for you.

1. One rule	*Many rules*
2. One court	60 ....
3. A game	31 ....
4. A player	Many ....
5. A state	30 ....

When we tell one person about what another person is doing, we usually add *s* to the verb in the sentence. This is called making the verb agree with the subject.

He works hard.
She works hard.
James works hard.
His father works hard.

NOTE: We do not put an *s* on *work* when we say *I work* or *you work.*

B. Change the verb in italics to agree with the subject in each sentence.

1. James Adoa *shake* his head.
2. He *come* from the African country of Uganda.
3. James *make* $80 a month.
4. He *send* money home to his father.
5. His mother *want* good things for her son.

EXPRESSING YOURSELF

1. Why is James Adoa working so hard to bring basketball to Uganda? How does he think it will help his people?
2. Find Uganda, Kenya, Tanzania, and Zambia on a map of Africa. What do you know about these new African nations?
3. Adoa says that American kids should "appreciate" the U.S. What do you appreciate about our country? What do you find wrong with it?
4. In Uganda, soccer is the favorite game. Write a few sentences about your favorite game.

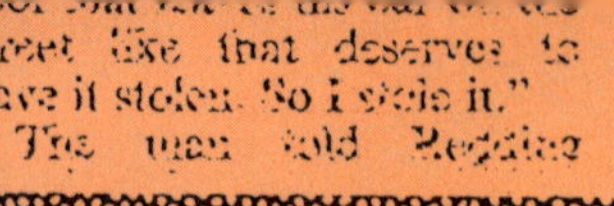

REVIEW OF LESSONS 21-25

FINDING THE MISSING WORD

The sentences below are followed by a list of *italicized* words. For each sentence, write the word that fits best in the blank. Use each word only once. (The number in parentheses tells you the number of the story in which the word was first used.)

1. The .... threw a player out of the game.
2. He had five years .... as a cab driver.
3. Juan is Spanish and speaks English with a Spanish ....
4. The sound of rock .... is not pleasing to me.
5. May I be of .... to you?
6. My father taught me a .... that I shall never forget.
7. A famous person usually has a very busy .... life.

8. I hate to .... the piano, but I love to play it.
9. He saw many rings at the .... store.
10. The basketball team works out in the ....

(a) *gym* (25)	(f) *lesson* (22)
(b) *referee* (21)	(g) *social* (24)
(c) *accent* (23)	(h) *practice* (25)
(d) *service* (24)	(i) *music* (23)
(e) *experience* (21)	(j) *jewelry* (22)

FINDING THE OPPOSITE

For each of the *italicized* words, choose the word on the right that is most nearly opposite. (The number in parentheses tells you the number of the story in which the word was first used.)

1. *accept* (21)	(a) refuse; (b) repeat; (c) take
2. *born* (23)	(a) cared; (b) lived; (c) died
3. *borrow* (22)	(a) lend; (b) send; (c) buy
4. *completed* (24)	(a) counted; (b) finished; (c) started
5. *forgotten* (23)	(a) past; (b) remembered; (c) taped
6. *lovely* (21)	(a) beautiful; (b) kind; (c) ugly
7. *outdoor* (25)	(a) nearby; (b) indoor; (c) everywhere
8. *recognize* (24)	(a) arrest; (b) forget; (c) remember
9. *taught* (25)	(a) reached; (b) thought; (c) learned
10. *usual* (22)	(a) simple; (b) sad; (c) strange

UNSCRAMBLING THE WORD

Each of the definitions below is followed by a scrambled word that fits the meaning. Unscramble the letters to find the word. (The number in parentheses tells you the number of the story in which the word was first used.)

1.	students in the last year of high school (21)	RESSION
2.	about the mind (24)	LAMENT
3.	two-legged outer garment (22)	SNAPT
4.	small bits of glass (22)	SEBAD
5.	clothing worn by the member of a team or other group (25)	INFORUM
6.	type of football game (25)	RECCOS
7.	shape (21)	GIFURE
8.	eating place (22)	STAURRANET
9.	person who digs for coal (23)	NEMIR
10.	small simple house (23)	NICAB

FINDING THE RIGHT MEANING

For each of the *italicized* words, choose its correct meaning from the choices on the right. (The number in parentheses tells you the number of the story in which the word was first used.)

1. *accident* (23) — (a) lucky happening; (b) unlucky happening; (c) happy happening

2. *advise* (24)	(a) to lie about; (b) to tell about; (c) to tell what should be done
3. *appreciates* (25)	(a) hates; (b) operates; (c) enjoys
4. *beard* (22)	(a) cold drink; (b) wild animal; (c) hair on the face
5. *center* (24)	(a) middle; (b) edge; (c) beginning
6. *coach* (21)	(a) trainer; (b) referee; (c) player
7. *courts* (25)	(a) places where people eat; (b) places where some sports are played; (c) places where players dress
8. *explosion* (23)	(a) a blowing up; (b) a speeding up; (c) a slowing down
9. *neatly* (22)	(a) orderly; (b) dirty; (c) poorly
10. *yelled* (21)	(a) whispered; (b) shouted; (c) talked

26. NINE-FOOT WOMAN

YOU ARE FIVE FEET TALL. THEN YOU GROW UNTIL YOU'RE SIX FEET TALL. YOU FEEL PRETTY GOOD. THEN YOU REALIZE THAT YOU ARE STILL GROWING . . . YOU'RE SEVEN FEET TALL . . .

WOULD YOU BE ABLE TO LEAD A HAPPY LIFE?

ALLAHABAD, India, Chronicle Foreign Service – A 27-year-old *peasant* is *wandering* the streets of Indian towns because no one wants to give her *shelter*. There are thousands of poor begging in this country, but Rasmanjari Rani is unwanted for a strange reason.

Rasmanjari is nearly nine-feet tall—one of the tallest women in the world.

When she went to a poor house the other day, the *priest* locked the door after one look at her.

"Maybe he thought I was a *witch,*" the dark-eyed woman said. Without any hate she told about her experiences.

Until three years before, Rasmanjari was of *normal height.* She had been married for many years. There were no children, but she and her husband were happy.

Suddenly, Rasmanjari started growing taller. In two or three months, she added four to five *inches* to her height. "Everyone in the village saw the change. I was *stared* at and made fun of. When I went to shop, children would follow me *chanting,* 'Tall woman, tall woman, you are like the mango tree.' I was even stoned once by some old women."

By last year Rasmanjari was almost nine-feet tall. There was no end to the poor woman's bad luck. Her husband had left her. Her brothers' wives turned against her. They said that she was *evil.* They blamed the death of a child in the family on her. One night she took what she owned and began wandering.

Doctors said she had an illness in the part of the body that controls growth. They said there was no cure. "The doctors do not think I will live many more years," she says simply.

"I hope the end comes soon. I am not afraid of death. I look forward to it," she said, drying her red and yellow sari * on the banks of the Ganges River.

—SAN FRANCISCO CHRONICLE

* sari – a dress worn by Indian women.

CHECK YOUR UNDERSTANDING

1. Rasmanjari began to grow again
   (a) after she got married.
   (b) when a priest called her a witch.
   (c) when her husband left her.
2. Rasmanjari's sisters-in-law
   (a) tried to help her.
   (b) blamed the death of a child on her.
   (c) gave her money for the doctors.
3. Rasmanjari is not afraid to die because
   (a) everyone has to die sometime.
   (b) it will end her suffering.
   (c) her husband will be able to marry again.
4. The doctors said that
   (a) she will live many years.
   (b) she had an illness in the part of the body that controls growth.
   (c) they will cure her in a few years.
5. Another title that would best explain the main idea of this story is:
   (a) How to Grow Tall
   (b) A Family of Giants
   (c) Problems of a Giant

FIND THE MISSING WORD

In your notebook, complete the following sentences with words from the story. You may look back at the story.

1. Rasmanjari is a 27-year-old .... wandering the streets.
2. Rasmanjari is unwanted for a strange ....: she is nearly nine-feet tall.
3. Rasmanjari was of normal ....

until three years ago.

4. In two or three months, she grew four to five ....

5. Everyone in the village .... at her when she walked by.

FIRST THINGS FIRST

Arrange these events in the order in which they really happened to Rasmanjari Rani.

1. She began wandering the streets of Indian towns.
2. She was locked out of a poor house.
3. Her husband left her.
4. She was married for many years.
5. She suddenly started to grow.

IMPROVING YOUR VOCABULARY

Fill in the blank space in each sentence in Column A with the word from Column B that fits best. Use each word in Column B only once.

A	B
1. We took .... from the rain in an old cabin.	(a) evil
	(b) stared
2. It was a .... March day, windy and cold.	(c) normal
	(d) shelter
3. She looked so much like my friend Juanita that I .... at her for a whole minute.	(e) height

4. His .... was five feet, ten inches.
5. It is .... to turn against someone because she is not like everyone else.

WORD BUILDING

Word Endings

A. Make the verb in italics agree with the subject.

1. Rasmanjari *remember* when she was normal.
2. James Adoa *see* a uniform on every player.
3. The young social worker *work* hard.
4. He *wear* faded pants and Indian beads.
5. When my father goes to work, my mother *wonder* whether he will ever come back.

When we want to show that someone owns something, we usually use a short cut. We add *'s* (*apostrophe s*). For example, if your friend owns a car, you say my friend*'s* car. Or if you want to talk about the uniform of a basketball player, you say the basketball player*'s* uniform.

BUT if a word ends in *s*, do *not* add *'s* to it. Add only an apostrophe to it: boys' names NOT boys*'s* names.

B. Change the words in italics to show ownership. The first one is done for you.

1. I went to my *husband* house. *husband's*
2. There was no end to the poor *girls* luck.
3. The *doctor* report said there was no cure.
4. I was a coal *miner* daughter.
5. The children opened the *witch* door.

EXPRESSING YOURSELF

1. Rasmanjari says she looks forward to death. What could you say to her to make her want to live?
2. Instead of feeling sorry for the poor woman, many people were angry at her. They made fun of her, threw stones, and blamed her when things went wrong. Why was she given such bad treatment?
3. Write a paragraph about someone you know who is different from most people. Tell whether that person has been treated well or badly by others.
4. Does this story remind you of any other stories in this book? Why?

27. A MAN WITH A HEART

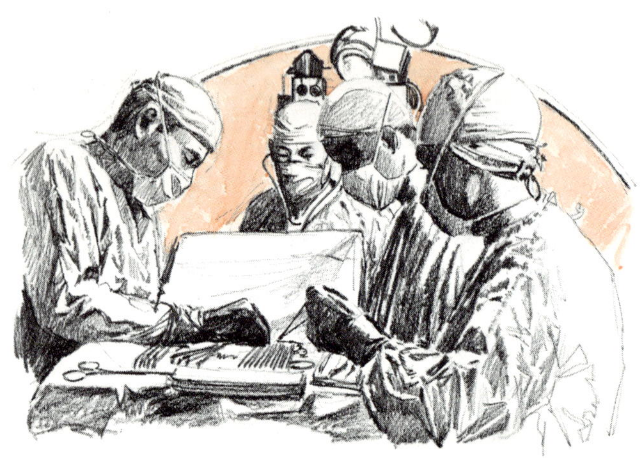

MANY NEW HEART OPERATIONS HAVE BEEN DONE BY DOCTORS. SUPPOSE YOU ARE ALIVE BECAUSE SOMEONE GAVE HIS HEART TO YOU.

WHAT WOULD YOU WANT TO DO WITH THE REST OF YOUR LIFE?

INDIANAPOLIS, Ind. – "The idea of being needed–that's the *reward* for me." That is how Louis B. Russell tells why his life is important.

Louis B. Russell is a man who knows what it means to have hope. On August 24, 1968, he received the heart of a 17-year-old boy who had just been killed. He was the 34th person in history to receive a second heart. He was the first black man to get one, though many black people had often given their hearts.

Seeing Mr. Russell today, you would not think his family life is different from that of any other person. He works full time as a shop teacher. He thinks that the most beautiful thing that happened to him was the *birth* last year of his first grandchild, Traci Lea.

His wife still worries about his *health,* but not as much as she did the first year he had his new heart. "Then," he complains, "everytime I fixed my tie, she asked me if I had a pain."

Mrs. Russell often goes with her husband on his speaking *tours,* from which they often bring home *awards.* In his new *role* he tries to sell hope to other sick people. "I give *encouragement,"* he says simply.

People call all the time. "I got a call from California at 3 A.M. from a man who said his brother was going in for a *lung* operation. They're *grabbing* for any hope," Russell said.

"I tell them whatever they want to hear. I encourage them that it's going to turn out well. I guess they call me because I have been so close to death."

"I went to see a woman with cancer not far from here. I only spent a half hour with her, but her family called me and said I gave her so much *courage."*

Louis B. Russell is a man with a second heart but what a great, grand heart it is.

—LOUISVILLE COURIER-JOURNAL

CHECK YOUR UNDERSTANDING

1. Louis B. Russell is a
   (a) heart doctor.
   (b) shop teacher.
   (c) famous priest.
2. He thinks that the most beautiful thing that ever happened to him is
   (a) the gift of a new heart.
   (b) giving up smoking.
   (c) the birth of his first grandchild.
3. The most important reward for Louis B. Russell is
   (a) helping others.
   (b) working hard.
   (c) raising his children.
4. Louis B. Russell tries to help people by
   (a) giving them money.
   (b) telling them what they want to hear.
   (c) telling them about his own troubles.
5. Another title that would best explain the main idea of this story is:
   (a) Doctors Succeed with New Hearts
   (b) A Successful Shop Teacher
   (c) A Thankful Man Who Helps Others

FIND THE MISSING WORD

In your notebook, complete the following sentences with words from the story. You may look back at the story.

1. Louis B. Russell's .... in life is the idea of being needed.

2. His wife still worries about his ...., but not as much as she did the first year.
3. Mr. Russell tries to sell hope to other sick persons in his new .... in life.
4. Mr. Russell said that people who call him and need help are .... at hope.
5. Mr. Russell has won many .... for the talks he has given.

FIRST THINGS FIRST

Arrange these events in the order in which they really happened to Louis B. Russell.

1. He was the 34th person in history to receive a second heart.
2. He suffered from a bad heart.
3. He gives hope to sick people.
4. He complained that his wife worried about him every time he fixed his tie.

IMPROVING YOUR VOCABULARY

Fill in the blank space in each sentence in Column A with the word from Column B that fits best. Use each word in Column B only once.

A	B
1. Dennis played the ...... of the hero in the class play.	(a) courage (b) encouragement
2. My cousin Wanda gave .... to a six-pound baby girl.	(c) birth (d) health (e) role

3. Thanks to Coach Nelson's ...., Rick is now a star football player.
4. Good .... habits prevent illness.
5. Walter had the .... of a lion; he was afraid of nothing.

WORD BUILDING

Word Endings

Change the words in italics to show ownership.

1. The *girl* jokes were very funny.
2. *Ota* poem is remembered with pleasure.
3. *Rick* first job was dangerous.
4. *Russell* life is not different from any other life.
5. Many *students* awards were earned by the girls.

Contractions

When we speak or write, we often make *contractions*. A contraction is a word, like *don't,* made by joining two words together. In such words, letters are often left out. When we write words that have been joined, we use an apostrophe to take the place of any missing letters. For example, *is not* becomes *isn't* by joining the two words together and replacing the *o* in *not* with an apostrophe.

A. In each sentence, join the words in italics and replace the *o* in *not* with an apostrophe.

1. I *do not* know if Americans appreciate what they have.
2. Living in Uganda *is not* easy.
3. She *does not* feel well.
4. Loretta *has not* forgotten the people back home.
5. Basketball coaches *are not* happy with a girl referee.

B. Here are words you know that have been joined together. Separate the words and add the letter or letters that an apostrophe was used for. The first one is done for you.

1. *Let's* play ball. *Let us.* (The apostrophe takes the place of *u*)
2. *I'm* not going to make it.
3. *You're* not finding this work hard.
4. If he is not ready, *we'll* leave without him.
5. *I've* answered too many questions.

EXPRESSING YOURSELF

1. Louis B. Russell has been helped to a new life. How can he help others?
2. Suppose that doctors found ways to replace every diseased part of the human body. Would you want to live to be 150 years old? Why might some people say no to that question?

3. For Mr. Russell, the idea of being needed is his greatest reward in life. What would be yours?

4. Write a letter to Louis B. Russell telling him why you admire him. (Or, write a letter to another person you admire.)

28. BEAR KILLED TO SAVE MAN

"PLEASE DON'T FEED OR ANNOY THE ANIMALS." WHY DOES THE ZOO HAVE SUCH SIGNS?

ONE MAN FOUND OUT THE HARD WAY.

It was a warm, *pleasant* day at the Central Park Zoo. There was a *crowd* of people in front of Skandy's cage. Skandy was the zoo's 800-pound *polar* bear.

Suddenly a man jumped over a three-foot fence that stood between the cage and the crowd. He stuck his hand between the *bars* of the cage.

The polar bear came and quickly grabbed his hand.

Policeman Charles Dlugokicki ran to the cage when he heard the *screams*. "There must have been 200 people there," he said. "They were all yelling. I could see this man fighting to get his arm away from the bear."

The policeman said he jumped over the rail and tried to push the bear away from the man.

"Nothing worked," he said. "Then I took out my gun and fired into the air. I hoped that the animal would let go. *Instead,* it pulled in more of the man's hand."

Then Eddie Rodriquez, the lionkeeper at the zoo, went to help the policeman. He started pushing the bear with a stick, but that didn't work either. "Then," the policeman said, "I made up my mind I'd have to *shoot* the bear."

The policeman fired into the left side of the animal's chest. The bear let go of the man's hand. He staggered back and fell dead. The man was taken to the hospital where he was put under care for *shock* and cuts.

A man from the zoo said that Skandy had been very easy to get along with. "But," he said, "you know how caged animals are. Put a toy before them and they'll take it right in their mouths."

Mr. Rodriquez said: "This man was *bothering* the animals. I just chased him away from another place. He was teasing them."

A man who watched the whole thing said,

"It was pretty bad. The bear would not let go and the man was screaming. He had been teasing the bear. He must have been *crazy*."

—NEW YORK TIMES

CHECK YOUR UNDERSTANDING

1. When the man jumped over the fence
  (a) the policeman yelled at him.
  (b) the polar bear moved back.
  (c) he pushed his hand between the bars of the cage.

2. The first thing the policeman did was
  (a) shoot the bear.
  (b) try to push the bear away from the man.
  (c) fire his gun into the air.

3. The lionkeeper
  (a) started pushing the bear with a stick.
  (b) fired his gun, too.
  (c) did not try to help the policeman.

4. Mr. Rodriquez said that
  (a) Skandy was hard to get along with.
  (b) the man was bothering the animals.
  (c) the policeman should not have killed the bear.

5. Another title that would best explain the main idea of this story is:
  (a) Policeman Saves Man Who Had Teased Bear
  (b) Helping Your Fellow Man Is Not Always Easy
  (c) A Pleasant Day at the Central Park Zoo

FIND THE MISSING WORD

In your notebook, complete the following sentences with words from the story. You may look back at the story.

1. It was a warm, ... day.
2. He pushed his hand between the .... of the cage.
3. The policeman ran to the cage when he heard the .... of the crowd.
4. He was put under care for .... and cuts.
5. Mr. Rodriquez said, "This man was .... the animals."

FIRST THINGS FIRST

Arrange these events in the order in which they really happened.

1. The crowd started to scream.
2. A man jumped over a fence that stood between Skandy's cage and the people.
3. The man was taken to the hospital.
4. The policeman had to shoot the bear.
5. The bear grabbed the man's hand.

IMPROVING YOUR VOCABULARY

Fill in the blank space in each sentence in Column A with the word from Column B that fits best. Use each word in Column B only once.

29. SUPERMEX

PLAY FOR FUN, OR PLAY TO WIN?

CAN YOU DO BOTH?

Not long ago *golf* was thought to be a game for people with a lot of money. Today, golf is played by over 12 million Americans on more than 10,000 golf *courses*.

One of the great golfers of all time is Supermex. And when Supermex started golfing, he surely did not have much money. Supermex is Lee Trevino, Mexican-American and school dropout. He was brought up in Dallas, Texas, in a house that had no *electricity* or running water.

He is the first golfer ever to win the three most important golf *tournaments* in the same year.

The golf crowd loves to watch him. "There are a lot of people for me," Trevino says, "because there are more poor people than rich people. To the *fans* who watch me, I'm someone who worked hard and made it. Sure I go out of my way to talk to them. They're my people."

His fans love his *wisecracks.*

FAN: Nice drive *!

LEE: What did you think you'd get from the U.S. Open ** winner – ground balls?

And "Black is beautiful, but brown is *cute.*"

Lee has fun while he makes money. Once he made everyone laugh at the start of an important round *** when he threw a toy *snake* at the golfer he was playing with. He talks and jokes all the time to the watching crowd. He says, "You only go around once in life–and you have to smell the *roses* as you go by."

Lee's secrets for winning golf are, "Stay loose" and "Practice." "I play every day," he says. "Even if I'm taking some time off, I'm out there beating balls. You've got to hit the ball in this game until your hands *bleed.*"

—TIME MAGAZINE

* drive – a long golf hit.
** U.S. Open – an important golf event.
*** round – 18 holes of golf.

CHECK YOUR UNDERSTANDING

1. Today, golf
(a) is played only by rich people.

(b) is played by more than 12 million Americans.
(c) is not a game Mexican-Americans can play.

2. Lee Trevino
   (a) is a college graduate.
   (b) was a poor boy in Dallas, Texas.
   (c) is not liked by golf fans.
3. Lee believes in
   (a) not talking to his fans.
   (b) not practicing.
   (c) having fun.
4. In the next to last paragraph, "You only go around once in life–and you have to smell the roses as you go by" means
   (a) you should love flowers.
   (b) you should get as much fun out of life as you can.
   (c) you have to take the good with the bad.
5. Another title that would best explain the main idea of this story is:
   (a) Poor Boy Becomes Great Golfer
   (b) A Game for Rich People
   (c) No Fun in Golf

FIND THE MISSING WORD

In your notebook, complete the following sentences with words from the story. You may look back at the story.

1. Not long ago .... was thought to be a game for people with a lot of money.
2. He is the first golfer ever to win the three biggest golf .... in the same year.

3. Trevino was brought up in a house that had no ....
4. "You've got to hit the ball in this game until your hands ...."
5. He threw a toy .... at the golfer he was playing with.

PROVE IT

When you make a statement or give an opinion, you should back it up with facts or examples. Each question below begins with a statement that comes from the story. Pick out the answer that *best* proves the statement by fact or example.

1. Lee Trevino is one of the great golfers of all time.
   (a) He is a Mexican-American.
   (b) His fans love his wisecracks.
   (c) He was the first golfer ever to win the three most important golf tournaments in the same year.
2. Lee Trevino was a poor boy.
   (a) He was brought up in a house that had no electricity or running water.
   (b) He was brought up in Dallas, Texas.
   (c) He was a school dropout.
3. Lee has fun while he plays golf.
   (a) He hits golf balls until his hands bleed.
   (b) He once jokingly threw a toy snake at a golfer he was playing with.
   (c) He loves flowers.
4. Lee believes in practice as a secret for winning golf.
   (a) He talks and jokes all the time to the watching crowd.

(b) He plays golf every day, even when he is taking time off.
(c) He won the U.S. Open tournament.

IMPROVING YOUR VOCABULARY

Fill in the blank space in each sentence in Column A with the word from Column B that fits best. Use each word in Column B only once.

A	B
1. Over 20,000 .... came out to watch the baseball game.	(a) electricity
2. Tina was a .... little girl.	(b) fans
3. The toy train works on	(c) roses
4. We saw a .... in the grass.	(d) snake
5. The .... begin to grow in late spring.	(e) cute

WORD BUILDING

Word Endings

A. Change each verb in italics to show past time.

1. I *work* a week ago.
2. They *watch* me this morning.
3. We *start* to play a year ago.

4. Louis Russell *receive* a new heart in 1968.
5. A woman *call* him last week.

When you add an ending beginning with a vowel (*-ed* and *-ing*) to a one-syllable word that ends in a consonant, you usually double the final consonant:

Word Ending With Consonant	+ Ending	= New Word With Double Consonant
grab	+ *ed*	= *grabbed*
grab	+ *ing*	= *grabbing*
beg	+ *ed*	= *begged*
beg	+ *ing*	= *begging*

EXCEPTION: You do not double the last consonant if a word ends in a double consonant, or, if a word has two vowels before the last consonant:

push	+	*ed*	=	*pushed*
need	+	*ed*	=	*needed*

B. Add *-ing* and *-ed* to each of these words. The first one is done for you.

1. shop	*shopping*	*shopped*
2. stab		
3. call		
4. lock		
5. need		
6. look		
7. yell		
8. stop		
9. rob		
10. slap		

EXPRESSING YOURSELF

1. Tell about a person from a poor family who made good.
2. Who is your favorite athlete? Why?
3. Lee's secrets for winning are "stay loose" and "practice." Write a paragraph giving your secrets for success–in sports, or any other activity.

30. FROM HERO TO HEROIN

ARE SOME PEOPLE MORE LIKELY TO BECOME DRUG ADDICTS THAN OTHERS?

WHY DID EVERYONE BELIEVE IT COULDN'T HAPPEN TO CLINT DICKENS?

HARRISBURG, Pa. (AP) – Clint Dickens was a heroin *addict*. When they found out, a lot of people still could not believe it. When they heard about the *lies*, when they saw the broken body, their words went something like this: "He's the last kid you would have thought. . . ."

At McCaskey High School in nearby Lancaster, Dickens had been a school *hero*. He was *president* of the student body and an all-star football player.

At 6 feet 2 and 210 pounds, he was fast and strong. Many college coaches were *eager* to have this good-looking young man on their teams. Scholarships rolled in.

But today when he walked through the doorway of a drug-help center, he was 30 pounds lighter. A police *detective* said he looked like a dirty-smelling dog.

For more than a year he had brought only trouble and *grief* to himself and to others. He lied. He stole. When he was 22, his wife left him. He did not work. He only worried about where the next bag was coming from. When the police picked him up the last time, he was living in a dirty rooming house.

"I didn't care," he said. "I was very blue. Nothing mattered. My clothes hung on me. It didn't make any *difference*. I never wore anything but Wranglers and a dirty old T-shirt anyway."

Clint's problems started with marijuana * in his second year at Virginia Union University. He was there on a football scholarship.

"I started with marijuana," he said, "because I was too proud to say no. I was with some friends. They said they had something for me to try. We rolled a joint.** I wanted them to think of me as a man. We passed the joints around. I became part of the group."

Later Clint became a heroin *** addict. He started with *nickel* ($5.00) bags and went to larger and larger ones. He came to *depend* on it.

Yet he had not wanted to use heroin at first. "In August I went to New York to get some pot. In an apartment two guys asked me if I wanted to shoot. I told them no. 'O.K.,' they said, 'then just sniff it.' I did and I got high fast. I was a little afraid. But I thought that if I got this high just sniffing, what a high I would get if I shot! So I started."

* marijuana (or pot) – the dried leaves of a hemp plant that are rolled into a cigarette. People who smoke it get "high."

** joint–a marijuana cigarette.

*** heroin – an illegal habit-forming drug that causes you to get very "high."

"I let a lot of people down," says Dickens. "I had always loved my parents. I loved football. I was a high school hero. I had a lot going for me, and I blew it."

—MILWAUKEE JOURNAL

CHECK YOUR UNDERSTANDING

1. Clint Dickens began to smoke marijuana because
- (a) he wanted to show his friends that he was a man.
- (b) he knew it made him calm before a game.
- (c) it cost only a nickel.

2. When people heard that Clint became a heroin addict, they
- (a) said he would be the first kid to do something like that.
- (b) told his father and football coach.
- (c) could not believe it.

3. Clint began to lie and steal when
- (a) his father wouldn't give him money.
- (b) he wanted to bet on a football game.
- (c) he needed money for heroin.

4. Clint went to Virginia Union University because
- (a) he was president of his high school class.
- (b) he received a football scholarship.
- (c) he would be able to play pro basketball there.

5. Another title that would best explain the main idea of this story is:
- (a) Football Star Loses to Drugs
- (b) A Football Hero
- (c) How to Keep Calm

FIND THE MISSING WORD

In your notebook, complete the following sentences with words from the story. You may look back at the story.

1. Clint Dickens is a heroin . . . .
2. He was . . . . of the student body in high school.
3. A police . . . . said that he looked like a dirty-smelling dog when he picked him up.
4. Clint brought a lot of trouble and . . . . to himself and others.
5. Once he started using heroin, he came to . . . . on it.

FIRST THINGS FIRST

Arrange these events in the order in which they really happened to Clint Dickens.

1. He was an all-star high school football player.
2. He became very blue and nothing mattered to him except getting heroin.
3. He went to a university in Virginia.
4. The first time he used heroin was in New York City.
5. He had already lost 30 pounds when he went for help to a drug-help center.

IMPROVING YOUR VOCABULARY

Fill in the blank space in each sentence in Column A with the word from Column B that fits best. Use each word in Column B only once.

A	B
1. There was a big .... in height between the two boys.	(a) hero
2. Rico was .... to win a scholarship to college.	(b) difference
3. Sam became a .... when he saved the girl from the fire.	(c) depend
4. Karen was elected .... of her class.	(d) president
5. Tom is a person you know you can .... on.	(e) eager

WORD BUILDING

Word Endings

A. Add *-ing* and *-ed* to each of these words.

1. plan	**6.** own
2. pick	**7.** add
3. roll	**8.** kid
4. ask	**9.** tip
5. trap	**10.** turn

When you add *-ing* to a one-syllable word that ends in a silent *e,* you first drop the *e* before you add the ending. For example, to make the word *living* from *live,* you drop the silent *e* before adding *-ing*.

B. Add *-ing* to each of these words. The first one is done for you.

1. fire	*firing*	**6.** cause
2. chase		**7.** blame
3. hope		**8.** please
4. tease		**9.** rule
5. hate		**10.** owe

Review

A. Add *-ing* to each of these words.

1. walk
2. come
3. live
4. tap
5. help

B. In each sentence, change the italicized word to show past time.

1. As she *walk* through the doorway, she felt strange.
2. The players *roll* in the mud until no one could tell them apart.
3. The girls *tease* the boys.
4. The bear *grab* the hand of the man who was teasing him.
5. You will be *test* for the last time in this section.

C. Join the words in italics and replace the missing letter with an apostrophe.

1. It *is not* easy to tell a good joke.
2. It *does not* matter whether you win or lose.
3. Why *are not* more people sad when they lose?
4. *They are* afraid they will not be liked.
5. After all, *is not* it true that nobody loves a loser?

D. Change the words in italics to show ownership.

1. the *peasant* wandering
2. the *bear* grip
3. the *golfer* wisecracks
4. an *addict* death
5. the *parents* grief

EXPRESSING YOURSELF

1. What would you say was Clint Dickens' biggest weakness?
2. Do you think Clint's use of marijuana led to his becoming a heroin addict? Explain.
3. You are at a party and someone passes around marijuana cigarettes. Also, in another part of the room a few people are getting ready to use heroin. "How about you?" a friend asks. "Are you chicken?" How would you answer him?
4. Write a paragraph about someone you know or heard about who had everything going for him and then "blew it."

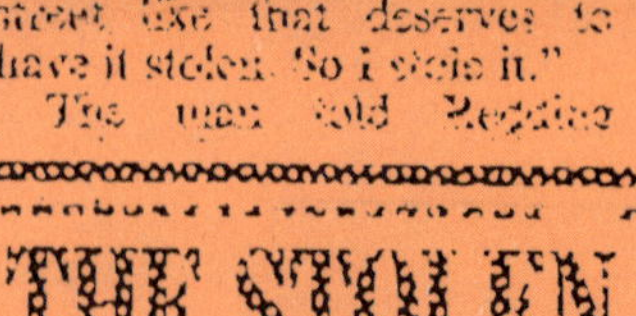
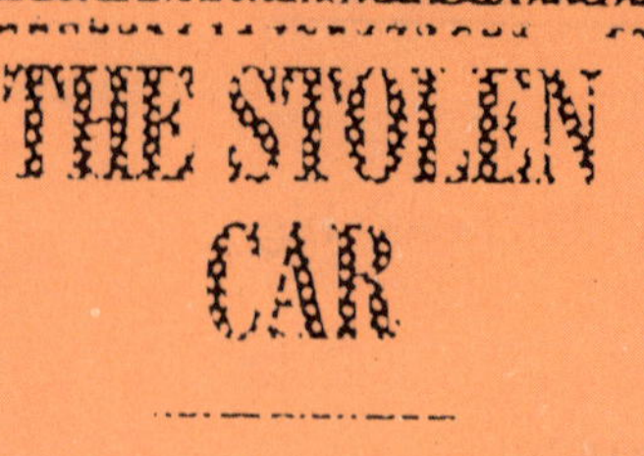

REVIEW OF LESSONS 26-30

FINDING THE MISSING WORD

The sentences below are followed by a list of *italicized* words. For each sentence, write the word that fits best in the blank. Use each word only once. (The number in parentheses tells you the number of the story in which the word was first used.)

1. All of the baseball fans were .... the same thing: "We want a hit! We want a hit!"
2. They found .... from the rain under an old bridge.
3. Patients need a lot of .... to get well.
4. An Emmy .... is given to television stars.
5. As he touched the two wires, he got a sudden ....
6. Over 20,000 persons were in the .... to watch the President of the United States.
7. Maria was a .... baby with curly hair.

8. Without ...., you could not watch TV.
9. Abraham Lincoln was our sixteenth ....
10. Felix received a .... for finding Mr. Castillo's wallet.

(a) *shock* (28)
(b) *electricity* (29)
(c) *chanting* (26)
(d) *reward* (27)
(e) *crowd* (28)
(f) *encouragement* (27)
(g) *president* (30)
(h) *shelter* (26)
(i) *cute* (29)
(j) *award* (27)

FINDING THE OPPOSITE

For each of the *italicized* words, choose the word on the right that is most nearly opposite. (The number in parentheses tells you the number of the story in which the word was first used.)

1. *birth* (27) — (a) life; (b) death; (c) fear
2. *bothering* (28) — (a) annoying; (b) worrying; (c) pleasing
3. *difference* (30) — (a) ending; (b) reward; (c) sameness
4. *eager* (30) — (a) wanting; (b) uncaring; (c) seeing
5. *evil* (26) — (a) bad; (b) good; (c) fun
6. *grabbing* (27) — (a) freeing; (b) seizing; (c) crawling
7. *grief* (30) — (a) sadness; (b) happiness; (c) tenderness
8. *health* (27) — (a) science; (b) sickness; (c) law
9. *lies* (30) — (a) truths; (b) wrongs; (c) opinions

10. *normal* (26) (a) usual; (b) unusual; (c) usable

UNSCRAMBLING THE WORD

Each of the definitions below is followed by a scrambled word that fits the meaning. Unscramble the letters to find the word. (The number in parentheses tells you the number of the story in which the word was first used.)

1.	man of the church (26)	STRIPE
2.	type of bear (28)	RAPOL
3.	five cents (30)	CLIKEN
4.	to fire a gun (28)	THOSO
5.	poor farmer (26)	SANPEAT
6.	to count on help from (30)	PEDEND
7.	parts of the body used for breathing (27)	GNULS
8.	travels from place to place (27)	ROUST
9.	to lose blood (29)	DEBEL
10.	place for games or races (29)	SOURCE

FINDING THE RIGHT MEANING

For each of the *italicized* words, choose its correct meaning from the choices on the right. (The number in parentheses tells you the number of the story in which the word was first used.)

1. *addict* (30) (a) person who sells drugs; (b) person who mixes drugs; (c) person who can't do without drugs

2. *courage* (27)	(a) frightened feeling; (b) brave feeling; (c) angry feeling
3. *detective* (30)	(a) army officer; (b) special policeman; (c) movie star
4. *instead* (28)	(a) in need of; (b) in place of; (c) in thanks for
5. *pleasant* (28)	(a) thankful; (b) enjoyable; (c) poor
6. *role* (27)	(a) part; (b) piece; (c) bread
7. *scream* (28)	(a) cover; (b) look; (c) yell
8. *stared* (26)	(a) looked at; (b) became known; (c) stepped down
9. *tournaments* (29)	(a) children's games; (b) sports contests; (c) square dances
10. *wandering* (26)	(a) turning around; (b) thinking about; (c) moving about

WRAPPING IT UP:
A REVIEW OF LESSONS 16-30

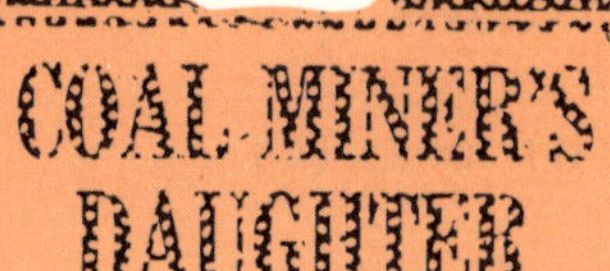

COAL MINER'S DAUGHTER

HOW DOES FOLK SINGER LORETTA LYNN FEEL ABOUT THE PEOPLE FROM "BACK HOME"?

"I was born a coal miner's daughter, in a cabin on a hill in Butcher Holler."

That's how life began for Loretta Lynn. She left the coal fields of Eastern Kentucky to become a country music star. But she hasn't forgotten the people back home. She hasn't forgotten how poor they are, or how dangerous it is to work the mines.

So she's busy now, getting together a big country music show. All the money from the show will go to the wives and children of 38 miners killed two months ago in a mine explosion.

Loretta Lynn still talks and sings with a strong mountain accent. She wrote a hit song, "Coal Miner's Daughter." That song is the story of her own early life in Kentucky.

"I grew up in Butcher Holler," she said. "My daddy was

Maybe he thou...
witch," the dark-eyed woman said. Without any hate she told about her experiences.

Until three years before, Rasmanjari was of normal height. She had been married for many years. There were no children, but she and her husband were happy.

Suddenly, Rasmanjari started growing taller. In two or three months, she added four to five inches to her height. "Everyone in the village saw the change. I was stared at and made fun of. When I went to shop, children would follow me chanting, 'Tall woman, tall woman, you are like the mango tree.' I was even stoned once by some old women."

By last year Rasmanjari was almost nine feet tall. There was no end to the poor woman's bad luck. Her husband had left her. Her brothers' wives turned against her. They said that she was evil. They blamed the death of a child in the family on her. One night she took what she owned and began wandering.

Doctors said she had an illness in the part of the body that controls growth. They said there was no cure. "The doctors do not think I will live many more years," she says simply.

"I hope the end comes soon. I am not afraid of death—I look forward to it," she said, drying her red and yellow sari on the banks of the Ganges

Orang...

Orange people? People
color of the orange you
A doctor told of a man
had come to him for help.
man had been living in Al
for three years. He tho
he was not getting enough
light there. He ate about
carrots a day. He dran
large can of tomato j
every three days. He also
lots of yellow vegetables.
Too many carrots, toma
and yellow vegetables ca
him to turn orange.
The cure was simple.
doctor told the man to

THE STOLE CAR

CANTON, Ohio (AP
One morning at the police
tion, Policeman Ed Red
received a call. The caller
he had just stolen a car.
"Is that so? How co
Redding asked.
"Well," said the man,
taking a walk. I see this
Its motor is running and
body is in it. I thought that
fool that leaves his car o
street like that deserve

FINDING THE MISSING WORD

Write the *italicized* word from below each sentence that fits best into the blank space.

1. If you want to .... famous, you must do something outstanding.
(a) *accept;* (b) *become;* (c) *begin;* (d) *enter*

2. Rick's .... as a secret policeman looking for drug addicts is dangerous.
(a) *accident;* (b) *poison;* (c) *job;* (d) *honesty*

3. My favorite subject is ....
(a) *poem;* (b) *spelling;* (c) *cloud;* (d) *hippie*

4. At .... 8 P.M. the basketball tournament will begin.
(a) *crazy;* (b) *exactly;* (c) *lovely;* (d) *shock*

5. Abe Lincoln was born in a log ....
(a) *polar;* (b) *shock;* (c) *cabin;* (d) *deserted*

6. Shot in the back, Louis .... to his horse and fell.
(a) *praised;* (b) *staggered;* (c) *recognized;* (d) *stared*

7. His friend ran from the .... store with a box of cornflakes.
(a) *grocery;* (b) *social;* (c) *blond;* (d) *address*

8. The storekeeper couldn't believe that his store had been ....
(a) *robbed;* (b) *stabbed;* (c) *shot;* (d) *became*

9. A newspaper .... asked the police some questions about the bank robbery.
(a) *miner;* (b) *reporter;* (c) *pajamas;* (d) *priest*

10. A .... watches the players to see that they don't break the rules.
(a) *referee;* (b) *doctor;* (c) *detective;* (d) *gym*

11. If you want a special job, it would help if you have ....

(a) *childhood;* (b) *circles;* (c) *experience;* (d) *shelter*

12. Does you girl friend expect to receive expensive .... ?

(a) *jewelry;* (b) *soccer;* (c) *usual;* (d) *money*

13. George speaks English with a Greek ....

(a) *explosion;* (b) *accent;* (c) *spelling;* (d) *beard*

14. I love listening to country - and - Western ....

(a) *shock;* (b) *electricity;* (c) *music;* (d) *thunderstorm*

15. Working as a waiter, Walter found out how to give customers good ....

(a) *practice;* (b) *service;* (c) *height;* (d) *seniors*

16. José likes to .... the guitar early in the morning.

(a) *practice;* (b) *reward;* (c) *golf;* (d) *bleed*

17. Ten seconds were left in the game as the crowd began .... , "10, 9, 8, 7, 6, . . ."

(a) *wandering;* (b) *rushing;* (c) *bothering;* (d) *chanting*

18. The team found .... from the rain in the dugout.

(a) *cabin;* (b) *shelter;* (c) *center;* (d) *money*

19. We shouted .... to Helen as she got up to bowl.

(a) *pollution;* (b) *pajamas;* (c) *lies;* (d) *encouragement*

20. Willie Mays received an .... for being the most valuable player in 1965.

(a) *award;* (b) *accent;* (c) *eager;* (d) *accident*

21. Don't open the back of your TV set because there is danger of electric ....
(a) *poison;* (b) *shock;* (c) *freeze;* (d) *rules*

22. The .... at some football games go as high as 100,000.
(a) *uniforms;* (b) *trumpets;* (c) *crowds;* (d) *health*

23. Her sister is a ...., blue-eyed baby.
(a) *nickel;* (b) *polar;* (c) *college;* (d) *cute*

24. In the United States the people choose a .... every four years.
(a) *coach;* (b) *state;* (c) *hippie;* (d) *president*

25. A funny man once said that the .... between two numbers is another number.
(a) *difference;* (b) *reward;* (c) *height;* (d) *encouragement*

FINDING THE OPPOSITE

For each of the *italicized* words, choose the word on the right that is most nearly opposite. (The number in parentheses tells you the number of the story in which the word was first used.)

1. *against* (19)	(a) under; (b) for; (c) over
2. *born* (23)	(a) died; (b) lived; (c) torn
3. *borrow* (22)	(a) send; (b) wrote; (c) lend
4. *boss* (19)	(a) friend; (b) referee; (c) worker
5. *clattering* (20)	(a) noisy; (b) banging; (c) quiet
6. *completed* (24)	(a) met; (b) began; (c) blamed
7. *deserted* (18)	(a) empty; (b) joined; (c) ate

8. *eager* (30) (a) bored; (b) bird; (c) wanting

9. *enters* (16) (a) leaves; (b) arrives; (c) attacks

10. *evil* (26) (a) trouble; (b) good; (c) everywhere

11. *forgotten* (23) (a) left; (b) found; (c) remembered

12. *grief* (30) (a) dark; (b) happiness; (c) sadness

13. *health* (27) (a) sickness; (b) well-being; (c) rich

14. *honest* (18) (a) best; (b) kind; (c) cheating

15. *lies* (30) (a) tries; (b) truths; (c) traps

16. *lovely* (21) (a) beautiful; (b) ugly; (c) bright

17. *married* (18) (a) single; (b) together; (c) family

18. *normal* (26) (a) good; (b) right; (c) unusual

19. *outdoor* (25) (a) indoor; (b) nearby; (c) away

20. *possible* (20) (a) maybe; (b) impossible; (c) complete

21. *praised* (16) (a) blamed; (b) thanked; (c) paid

22. *recognize* (24) (a) repeat; (b) forget; (c) remember

23. *son* (16) (a) blond; (b) daughter; (c) coach

24. *taught* (25) (a) learned; (b) trained; (c) repeated

25. *usual* (22) (a) exactly; (b) forgotten (c) strange

UNSCRAMBLING THE WORD

Each of the definitions below is followed by a scrambled word that fits the meaning. Unscramble the letters to find the word. (The number in parentheses tells you the number of the story in which the word was first used.)

1. to receive (21) — PACCET
2. troubling (28) — THEROBING
3. taking hold suddenly (27) — BINGBARG
4. belonging to me (17) — NIEM
5. person who digs for coal (23) — REIMN
6. made (17) — LITUB
7. hair on the face (22) — DREAB
8. to change into ice (20) — EZEFER
9. made free from harm (19) — VSDEA
10. man of the church (26) — STRIPE
11. poor worker-farmer (26) — PASTEAN
12. to begin to fight (19) — KATCAT
13. goes around (16) — SLRECIC
14. type of horn (16) — PRETTUM
15. the twelfth month (20) — CEMBERED
16. to count on for help (30) — PEDDEN
17. five cents (30) — LICKEN
18. students in last year of high school (21) — SORISEN
19. shape (21) — URFIGE
20. clothing worn by a baseball player, policeman, etc. (25) — MINUFOR
21. eating place (22) — AURRESTANT
22. dealing with the mind (24) — MALTEN
23. one of the 50 main parts of the United States (18) — TASTE

24. to lose blood (29) LEBED
25. type of football game (25) CROCES

FINDING THE RIGHT MEANING

For each of the *italicized* words, choose its correct meaning from the choices on the right. (The number in parentheses tells you the number of the story in which the word was first used.)

1. *accident* (23) (a) unlucky happening; (b) death; (c) change

2. *addict* (30) (a) person who sells drugs; (b) person who can't do without drugs; (c) person who runs a drug center

3. *advise* (24) (a) to tell what should be done; (b) to make a vise; (c) to tell a story

4. *appreciates* (25) (a) repeats; (b) enjoys; (c) hates

5. *center* (24) (a) place where people eat; (b) place where people gather; (c) place where people study

6. *coach* (21) (a) sports teacher; (b) team player; (c) referee

7. *courage* (27) (a) frightened feeling; (b) happy feeling; (c) brave feeling

8. *courts* (25) (a) places where some sports are played; (b) tennis games; (c) places to swim

9. *danger* (16) (a) sadness; (b) trouble; (c) safety

10. *decide* (19)	(a) to make fun of; (b) to make safe; (c) to make up one's mind
11. *detective* (30)	(a) policeman; (b) mailman; (c) lawyer
12. *explosion* (23)	(a) a letting down; (b) a beating; (c) a blowing up
13. *instead* (28)	(a) in place of; (b) inside; (c) outside
14. *neatly* (22)	(a) orderly; (b) crooked; (c) interested
15. *opinion* (18)	(a) what you think; (b) what you know; (c) what you want
16. *pleasant* (28)	(a) poor farmer-worker; (b) enjoyable; (c) cool
17. *pollution* (17)	(a) health; (b) dirt; (c) food
18. *realize* (18)	(a) to deserve; (b) to cause; (c) to understand
19. *reason* (19)	(a) end; (b) center; (c) cause
20. *role* (27)	(a) bread; (b) part; (c) roll
21. *rushing* (20)	(a) hurrying; (b) slowing; (c) pushing
22. *scream* (28)	(a) pain; (b) yell; (c) sniff
23. *stared* (26)	(a) looked; (b) climbed; (c) took
24. *tournaments* (29)	(a) crops; (b) contests; (c) circles
25. *wandering* (26)	(a) waiting around; (b) throwing out; (c) moving about